# OPENSIDE

# OPENSIDE

*My Journey to the Rugby World Cup*

## David Pocock

### with Lance Peatey

NEW
HOLLAND

First published in Australia in 2011 by
New Holland Publishers Pty Ltd
Sydney • Auckland • London • Cape Town

www.newholland.com.au

1/66 Gibbes Street Chatswood NSW 2067 Australia
218 Lake Road Northcote Auckland New Zealand
86 Edgware Road London W2 2EA United Kingdom
80 McKenzie Street Cape Town 8001 South Africa

National Library of Australia Cataloguing-in-Publication entry:
        Pocock, David, 1988-

        Openside : my journey to the rugby world cup / David Pocock.

        ISBN 9781742571782 (pbk.)

        Pocock, David, 1988-, Rugby Union football players--Australia--Biography.
        Rugby Union football--Tournaments.

        796.333092

Publisher: Fiona Schultz
Publishing manager: Lliane Clarke
Project editor: Jodi De Vantier
Designer: Kimberley Pearce
Production manager: Olga Dementiev
Printer: McPherson's Printing Group, Maryborough, Victoria

10 9 8 7 6 5 4 3 2

Follow New Holland Publishers on Facebook:
www.facebook.com/NewHollandPublishers
Twitter: @NewHollandAU

# Dedication

The profits from this book will go towards developing a more reliable income stream for EightyTwenty Vision, to help with any future work it does with communities.

So it is to the good people of Nkayi, Zimbabwe (the location of EightyTwenty's first partnership) that I would like to dedicate this book. I am always learning from these wonderful people who, despite having so little, work so hard and have so much joy for living. I hope I can one day repay them for the grace, dignity and humility they have shown me.

# Contents

# Acknowledgements

I am so aware of the wonderful people who have contributed wholeheartedly to my life—both in terms of my rugby development and, more importantly, the person I am and the person I am becoming. I hope that the way I have talked about these people in this book will go some way towards making them aware of my appreciation of their contribution's.

I'd like to make particular mention of my family—Mum, Dad, Mike and Steve—who have all sacrificed so much for me and never ask for any recognition. They've always been so willing to help. Emma, my best friend and wife, thanks for all your help with this project and also for how much I continue to learn from you. I enjoy our friendship—you are a delight.

There have been so many other people: teachers, coaches, medical staff, players and friends. I'd particularly like to thank Simon Gough from my days at Midlands Christian School, David Grogan, Tom Barker, Mark Stevenson, Tom Hillier, Ricky Nalatu and the late Roman Wojcieszuk from my days at Churchie, and Paul Carozza and Dean Benton from my time with the National Talent Squad at Ballymore. I'd also like to thank the two Johns (Mitchell and Mulvihill) for giving me an opportunity at the Force, as well as everyone else involved in my development since then.

I'd like to make a special mention of Luke O'Keefe, one of my closest friends and someone who has been such a big part of my life over the past six years. Thank you for being such a great friend—we have learnt a lot together. To Bec, Sam, Zac and Kalen—thanks for allowing me (and Emma) to be a part of your family. On the home front I'd also like to thank Ailsa, our housemate. You are an amazing woman and Emma and I love living with you.

There are some people I want to thank specifically for helping me with this project. I'd like to thank Lance Peatey, without whom this would have been an absolute nightmare. Lance spent hours working away at the manuscript—structuring, editing and fact-checking. I'm also incredibly grateful to his wife Katherine, who I'm sure spent a considerable amount of time looking for mistakes and making suggestions. From New Holland, I am particularly grateful to Jodi De Vantier. I'd also like to thank Karen Pickering for her valuable insights and feedback, her willingness to come on board at short notice and her love of the written word.

# Foreword

I had the privilege of first meeting David Pocock in January 2006, during the Western Force's inaugural pre-season training. What immediately impressed me was his desire to win and leave nothing undone. On one particular day, there was beach training and I observed experienced players, like Brendan Cannon, noticing the never-say-die attitude of David and his desire to win everything in those beach and paddle races.

What set David apart from his peers at the time was that he never just relied entirely on the professional rugby program to make him but rather was always looking for more ways to improve and be the best he could be. I remember the Force's first-ever warm-up game against the Cheetahs when I asked David's dad Andy for his consent for David to play (because I was breaking an ARU ruling at the time) and he said, 'John, if you think he is ready, then that's fine by me.'

My objective with that decision, after having observed this impressive young man, was to let him experience the level of rugby he was striving for and would ultimately excel in. He experienced a twenty-minute lesson and gained a black eye and belief immediately, so that when the time arrived he could influence the outcome with his strengths. He went on to play his debut against the Sharks in the final round-robin in Durban that year and was outstanding. It was a testimony to his ability to learn quickly. I thought it was fitting for David to debut in South

Africa and the excitement and energy he exuded in those contests remain a good memory for me. He relished the opportunity that was presented and outwardly showed no fear.

I remember sometimes knocking on David's door away on tour to talk to him, and would often find him pushing out some push-ups. His pro-activeness to his training and nutrition was a result of his awareness about understanding how to maximise his potential and prioritise his needs.

David is a leader in my mind and will eventually carry the official team role for club and country. I remember the Force playing the Crusaders in Christchurch in 2009 and they were down at half-time. Dave came to me in the shed—invigorated and animated at the same time—and stood face-to-face with me and challenged me to bring teammate Matt Hodgson on to pick up our tempo and ground threat. I also remember asking at late notice for him to speak at Hale Year 12's class—it ended up being a full school assembly and he had a fantastic message to pass on to the students.

When my own coaching credibility was in question, and being undermined by management, he would meet me for a coffee in Floreat and showed me great empathy, questioned superbly and formed an understanding of the situation beyond his years.

I believe one of his finest matches for the Western Force was in 2010 against the Crusaders in Perth. I had asked him and his fellow loose forwards to stand up and put a stake into the ground and not wait for the Rugby World Cup. They all responded incredibly. David loves and responds to a challenge.

Having now lived in South Africa and understanding more about the situation in Zimbabwe, I have an even greater respect for David's EightyTwenty Vision charity. I admire the way he gives back to the underprivileged. Even though he works hard and is deserving of his status in global rugby, he is still humble and recognises that he is privileged to be in the position and the country he is in and represents. I have never heard him judge others—which is a wonderful character trait and a true mark of a person. He stands in his power with great inner confidence.

I was thrilled to be invited to his marriage with Emma last Christmas. It was a very special day and a beautiful celebration of marriage with, again, great messages and lessons for all involved. At the time, I was going through a serious decision in my life and that particular service reminded me to be true to myself and those around me. With Dave, what you see is what you get—he's a very consistent man, showing conviction in his beliefs and is constantly true to himself.

At the Rugby World Cup 2011, there were a number of players who I have been associated with during their careers and lives from a young age. But I have to admit I watch David more than any one other player. To me, he demonstrated in that tournament the qualities that make him who he is. It did not matter how tough the situation, he remained true to what drives him and was willing to go to lengths other players will not.

David, you are truly destined to become one of the game's greats and, when the time is right and you can devote more of your focus to such things, you have the humbleness and self-worth to have a greater influence on socio-economic matters. Thank you for this opportunity to share with people what such a special person you are, not only to me but to whoever is fortunate to be in your presence.

John Mitchell
*All Blacks coach 2001–2003*
*Western Force coach 2006–2010*

# 1.

# Sowing Seeds
## Our farm in Zimbabwe and early rugby moulding

My first memory of the Rugby World Cup is Pieter Hendriks pumping his fist as he scored against Australia in the opening match of the 1995 tournament in South Africa. I have great memories of watching the 1995 final between the Springboks and All Blacks on TV at my grandfather's farm in the Lowveld in Zimbabwe— the plane flying over the stadium, Nelson Mandela being at the game, and the Springboks in the final.

'… van der Westhuizen to Stransky, Stransky for the drop goal'— straight through the posts. I can still remember my dad, Andy, throwing his empty coffee mug in the air in joy. What a day—that's Rugby World Cup!

I started playing rugby in Grade 3 at Midlands Christian School in Gweru, a city near the centre of Zimbabwe, in Midlands Province. I had been throwing a ball around for as long as I can remember though and Mum tells me I used to sleep with my rugby ball as a kid. There's a photo of me somewhere at about two months old trying to reach for a ball that was just out of my grasp—it was obviously a pretty strong impulse. Halfway through my first day of training with the Grade 3s, I was sent to train with the Grade 5s and I played in the Grade 5 Colts team for the rest of the year. I loved it. If we ever went anywhere—to a friend's house for dinner, my grandfather's farm for the weekend or away on holiday—the rugby ball would come with us. My two brothers and I would kick the grip off it and we'd play with the bald bladder-looking ball until the inevitable day when it was kicked too far or mis-kicked into a thorn tree.

People often ask me if I played rugby in Zimbabwe. Rugby is played in most schools there and it has always been very competitive and of a pretty decent standard. Zimbabwe played in the 1987 and 1991 Rugby World Cups but has failed to qualify since then. Top players have often moved south of the border to play rugby in South Africa or further afield. Notable Zimbabwean players include Adrian Garvey, Gary Teichman, Tendai 'the Beast' Mtawararira and arguably two of the fastest men in rugby—Tonderai Chavhanga and Takudzwa 'Zee' Ngwenya. Tonderai got six tries on debut for the Springboks, and Takudzwa scored that memorable 'try of the tournament' for the USA, when he outpaced Bryan Habana against the Springboks at the 2007 Rugby World Cup in France.

We were lucky enough to have a satellite dish out on our farm and could get South African TV, including Supersport, which showed every game for the Currie Cup, South Africa's regional competition. And I would try and watch *every* game. I used to spend hours and hours watching rugby. Whether it was Griquas v Eastern Province or a big clash like Western Province against Natal Sharks, I'd try and pick up little things that certain players did or moves that came off. I'd write them down and then try and use them for the school team. I didn't miss too many Springbok games either—often we would go to a friend's place where we'd have a big *braai* (barbeque) and watch the game in the evening. I will admit, though, that when there were a lot of people there I hardly ever watched the game on TV—the opportunity to play rugby out on the grass with my mates was far more appealing. These games inevitably started as touch rugby but soon morphed into full-on contact, complete with rucks and mauls, and grass burns to remember the game by. It was always a case of laying claim to being your favourite player, and then you got to play as him for the game. I usually got in early, telling everyone that I was Bob Skinstad.

I didn't grow up thinking, 'Wow, my family is a rugby family so I'll be good at it'. But my dad and my grandfather say that every generation had excelled. My pop (Mum's dad) was a keen rugby player and had a lot of talent, but chose to pursue his studies, becoming an Air Force pilot and then eventually building up a very successful citrus farm in Zimbabwe. The land was classified as 'unfit for human habitation' but he bulldozed it from bare thorn bushes and scrub anyway. I love listening to his stories of starting the farm, with so many unknowns, he was really just beginning with a dream and seeing where it would lead, building it slowly over time with a lot of hard work. My uncle now runs it, which has been a very tough job given the political and economic situation that Zimbabwe has been in for the last ten years.

My dad, Andy, was a very good rugby player in his day too, but he also chose to study and then move back to the family farm. Dad says that things were very different back then because rugby never offered you the option of making a living and it took second place once he, and I imagine many like him, left school. Even though he couldn't keep playing, Dad sure passed on that love of rugby to his sons.

I'm the oldest of three boys. Mike's about eighteen months younger than me and Steve is four years younger. They are such good brothers: always keen for an adventure, not afraid of a bit of competition and they both love the outdoors. I sometimes feel sorry for my mother, Jane, who had to live in a house with three boys and my father. But Dad always says, with a chuckle, 'Your mum's fine, Dave, she married well.'

My brothers and I were forever playing hockey or rugby in the backyard. Or we'd play WWF (after the World Wrestling Federation, not the World Wildlife Fund), a sort of wrestling free-for-all where we would practise moves that we had seen on TV, but this only happened when Mum would go into town without us. When Mum came home, we'd hastily put the cushions back on the couches. She'd ask us, 'Boys, have you been wrestling?' at which point we'd lie and say that we hadn't. We were terrible liars and I'm sure we didn't fool her. We were under strict instruction not to watch wrestling on TV. It was 'too violent' and got us 'too wound up'. I'm certain Mum knew full well that we wrestled (she had caught us more than a few times and it's hard to cover things up when it ends in tears or a blood nose) but she turned a blind eye.

Mike's not doing so much wrestling anymore—he has almost finished university. He's been studying construction management and got a job in the field after doing some prac work for a company. He's really the handiest, most helpful guy you'd ever meet. At his 21st birthday party, the guys who made speeches all spoke about Mike being there for them during the hard times in their lives—that's Mike through and through. Whenever I have a project at home that needs doing I'll send him photos and a flurry of questions about how best to make it happen and he always has the answers. Back on the farm in Zimbabwe I would spend hours devising traps to capture wild birds or monkeys or the genets that lived in our roof (I did release them, but it was a lot of fun). Mike would inevitably help with the building of the trap from a sketch meticulously drawn on graph paper to a trap ready to carry down the hill from our house to where we wanted to set it up.

Steve's the youngest. I sometimes forget how young he is because he's really mature for his age. He came over to Perth for a few months after finishing school at the end of 2009 and the beginning of 2010. He was at the Western Force Academy and doing really well. He's a bit taller than me and also played on the flank. It was so good getting to spend that time together and sort of get to know one another again after years of being separated by most of Australia. We had some great times swagging in Margaret River, skinny dipping at various Perth beaches at midnight, surfing and just hanging out. At the beginning of 2011, Steve found out he couldn't continue playing rugby because of a niggling back injury. It was a tough time for him. He ended up heading to Africa for a few months and spending time on our grandfather and uncle's game farm, which is next to their citrus farm. Steve was there when my uncle was arrested by the police and locked up for the night. My grandfather had received a 'letter of no interest' from the Zimbabwean government after he bought the farm, which means that the government wouldn't be forcing them off the land. However, with my uncle's arrest, it seemed they had changed their mind. My uncle and grandfather eventually won a case against the government in the High Court, allowing them to keep the farm. When Steve returned, he enrolled at uni, in psychology and anthropology, and has been studying and writing his own book about his experiences when we left Zimbabwe and the following years. He doesn't think he'll publish it but it is more just for him to get it all out and has been a somewhat therapeutic experience.

I think having three boys was just what Dad needed. He often says that when he got home on his motorbike from working on the farm we would often get him to kick 'up-and-unders' to us in the garden. 'Just 100 kicks Dad, only 100. Then we can go inside. Please, it's getting dark', we would beg him. My poor dad. He had amazing patience with us boys and spent a lot of time with us outdoors, whether it was kicking a rugby ball or playing hockey in the garden after school, or showing us how to de-worm sheep, or trusting us with the *bakkie* (ute) on the farm from when we were ten or eleven.

During my childhood on the farm, I kicked Joel Stransky's drop-goal through our makeshift home-made goalposts hundreds of times. Then I'd retrieve the ball from the chicken run if it was a really good strike or from the passionfruit vine or bamboo if it just made it over—we always argued about who would retrieve the ball from there. Because it was just next to the chicken run there were usually a few snakes hanging out to feast on eggs or one of my bantam chickens, or even one of the bigger layers if it was an African rock python. When it was a wayward kick, we would have to remove it cautiously from the bougainvillea, which sometimes meant a puncture in our already bald ball—rugby balls weren't cheap so we used to cut the stitching and patch the inner up with a bicycle puncture kit and then, with help from Mum, stitch the ball back together.

Despite all the time spent playing and practising, I hardly missed a game Western Province was in—they were my favourite team in the Currie Cup. Their team boasted players like Breyton Paulse, Pieter Rossouw (also known as Slaap Chips or 'the intercept king'), Robbie Fleck, Corne Krige, Braam van Straaten and, of course, Bob Skinstad—I loved watching him play. My second favourite team was Natal Sharks, mostly because my mum's brother, A.I., was such a die-hard Sharks supporter and they had a great brand of rugby. The Sharks included guys like the Rolls Royce of fullbacks, Andre Joubert, plus James Small, Gary Teichmann and the crunching defender Henry Honiball—the best defensive fly-half in world rugby, my dad and I would agree. We also enjoyed watching Kevin Putt, the feisty halfback, either 'helping' the referee or quarrelling with opposing players.

I spent hours with my dad and my brothers watching rugby. From a young age I had no real doubt in my mind that one day I would be out there—I would be playing in the Currie Cup, playing rugby for the Springboks. Imagine playing for Western Province in the Currie Cup? Imagine running out at Newlands? Imagine playing against a team like the Blue Bulls—'die Blou Bulle'? For my grandfather, who went to boarding school in Pretoria, the Bulls were his favourite team. Maybe he would come and watch me?

I daydreamed about it quite a bit. There were no limits to my dreams and I am very grateful that my parents never once said I should be realistic or that I was being silly dreaming such things. I went from being an ardent Springbok supporter to following the Wallabies and wanting to play for them one day. Desperately wanting to play for them. I eventually became obsessed about doing everything I could to improve as a rugby player and eventually became so focused on my training and eating Mum took me to see a psychologist because I had become impossible to get through to. This didn't really help so Mum took me to a sports dietician and she helped me readjust the way I thought about eating and become less focused on being so lean. It seems very odd thinking about it now, but, of course, that's not the whole story.

My dad was a farmer, but he was also a teacher, and someone who set high standards for himself and the work he did on the farm. This inevitably gave us a very disciplined upbringing. I clearly remember him passionately explaining (and, at times, shouting) at the foreman and other workers back on the farm in Zimbabwe about doing 'half-jobs'. Half-jobs were unacceptable. Fences had to be straight, tomato trellises had to be made properly, rows should be dead straight and even the seed beds had to be set out correctly. Dad and the workers had this saying on the farm, 'number one in Zimbabwe', and that's what they strove to achieve. Mum worked hard too, looking after the accounts and books and keeping us three boys fed and under control. 'If you're going to do something, do it properly,' Dad used to say, and Mum would back him up.

We were never pushed to do sport or extracurricular activities—but if we committed to something, Mum would make sure that we saw it out to the end, no matter how many times it meant she drove to and from the farm along the strip road, then along the dodgy gravel road that never seemed to get graded, to take us to sport or choir or whatever it was.

Yes, I was actually in the school choir at primary school. I still haven't worked out whether nobody ever told me I couldn't sing in tune or if my voice just deteriorated (possibly something linked to puberty?). It's hard to say. Every now and then, my family takes great joy in bringing out an old video of Mike and me singing away in the choir. My younger brother, Steve, would never have taken part in anything like that, which possibly explains why girls at school found him so cute. Choir boys were not so appealing apparently. This was the least of my worries at school though—there was rugby to be played, motorbikes to be ridden and fun to be had on the farm. Attracting girls was fairly low down on the priority list. Low on the list at that stage anyway. It did change later on.

On the farm my brothers and I were largely left to our own devices. Mum tells us she was pretty uncomfortable with a lot of the things we did with our time, but knew that we had to test ourselves and that was part of growing up. She had grown up on a farm too and was not fussed by the inevitable blood and tears, and was always so comforting and looked after us when we got hurt. We had a huge tree in our garden that we used to 'abseil' down. We would borrow a few pulleys and rope from the workshop and hook them about five metres up the tree. One of us would tie the rope around our waist and the other two would pull—you'd go straight up the tree and then be let down as the two on the ground let the rope out again. The rope only snapped once— luckily it was when Steve was only a metre or two off the ground.

Mum and Dad encouraged us to use our initiative and make our own fun, hence the abundance of traps we used to set around the farm. We would go fishing in the reservoir, which was stocked with bream. I even bred up a nice little flock of bantam chickens and used to sell the eggs to the farm workers, which provided me with a little bit of pocket money. The highlight of our efforts—with help from the tractor driver, a block and tackle from the workshop and a lot of rope, as well as supervision from Dad—was hoisting a pre-welded tree house some eight metres into a huge Msasa tree in our yard. It was fairly dangerous—the only way up was to climb a rope ladder—but, boy, were we proud of that house.

We used to ride our bikes—Mike and Steve having taken their seats off entirely in order to reach the pedals—to where the sheep were kept at night and try to catch and ride the big rams. It was a sort of mini rodeo. Mike loves to remind me of the time one of the bigger rams, with fairly solid horns, charged and bucked me and landed me on my bum a few metres back. I looked back and Mike and Steve had darted up to the top of the fence and were laughing hysterically. I quickly joined them and we laughed some more together while I tried to get my breath back. In a similar incident I got overly confident around a 'tame' Brahman cow until she gave me a good buck, landing me flat on my back, much to the concern and then, after they were sure I was ok, amusement of my family.

We did go to school too—it wasn't always fun and adventures on the farm. We used to take shortcuts on the drive to school and I loved going through the sewerage works. When the sewage had been 'processed' they used to release it out onto some low-lying fields. It created a kind of wetland and there were always red-billed teals, a small member of the duck family, which I developed an affinity for. I was really into birds. My older cousin Tyler still rips me about my binoculars and bird book and how, whenever we used to go to a national park, I would keep a list of the birds we had seen and try to identify them by their call. I'd read up in the bird book and narrow down the choices until I was almost certain. I would then ask Dad or Pop for confirmation. They had both grown up on the land and were very knowledgeable.

During the rainy season, the sewage works would get flooded and the thick clay soils made it so boggy it was almost impossible to get through in a car. One day on the way to school, we were getting a lift in (we used to have a lift run with other farmers in the area to save fuel). On this occasion Steve, knowing full well that it was flooded, was saying that it should be fine to go via the sewage works. He managed to convince the driver to go that way and was so chuffed when we got stuck and had to radio back to the farm to get someone to pull us out—I can't remember if we got to school that day but it was a victory for Steve. He sat in the back chuckling while the poor neighbour was stressed that we'd be late for school.

This became almost the highlight of the school year—the one or two days a year when the rivers would flood. We would be cut off from town and would have to turn around at the sight of a mass of water flowing across the main road, to the cheering and singing of my brothers. We got to spend the day riding our bikes through puddles, catching tadpoles, looking for bullfrogs down near the dam, trying to build a raft on the small dam or helping dig trenches to stop the crops becoming too waterlogged.

Building a raft for the small dam that only filled up once or twice a year was one of our favourite things about summer on the farm—in Zimbabwe all the rains come in summer. The building process would inevitably drag out to a few days, with much deliberation about the design and then scrounging around the farm for spare milk bottles or any unused chemical container that would float. Our attempts were valiant, at best, but were never very successful. They always ended in a sinking raft and the three of us swimming like crazy to get to the shore to avoid the dreaded leeches latching on to us and sucking blood, although this was usually inevitable so after we'd reach the shore, we'd quickly start checking each other for leeches and pulling them off. All this usually happened in the company of friends. Our family has always seemed to attract friends to stay, sometimes for weekends, sometimes weeks, sometimes months or even years, and this has not changed to this day. When I go back to Brisbane I often joke that Mum and Dad's house is 'Hotel Pocock' because there is always someone staying there or popping in, or my brothers have mates over. I love it, though, and my parents taught me, and still teach me, the value of caring for people and opening your home to them.

On our days off or in the afternoon after school, we'd often spend hours kicking the rugby ball around the yard. One of us would stand up in the bush—behind the passionfruit vine and against the old chicken run that was looking the worse for wear, its rusty old tin roof leaning at a funny angle and the chicken wire patched up with scraps of wire—trying to avoid the bamboo because it was prickly and we had seen a python around there. The Rhode Island layers and my bantams took cover in the bougainvillea, while the ducks waddled down to the other end of the yard to escape the mayhem of the Pocock boys kicking and returning rugby balls. We got on pretty well, but bickered and fought a great deal over all the stupid little things brothers seem to fight about.

At nights we would plead with Dad to 'rough and tumble'. 'Please, only for a little while!' we would beg. Mum would always tell us to start settling down for bed time, but inevitably Mike, Steve and I would launch ourselves at Dad on the living room carpet (our carpet rugby field), as Dad tried to overpower us, tickling us. The older we got the more Dad had to work and by the time we were eight, eleven and twelve he had his hands full. But he was always so strong. He is our hero and we loved every minute we got to spend with him. A few years ago Dad told me that he remembered when he was a kid—and I imagine he was quite a handful—his father turning to him and saying, 'Son, I hope you have boys just like you'. I am very grateful my father has never said this to me as I cannot imagine having to raise three boys like my brothers and I—it would be tough going to say the least.

We grew up with a very clear understanding that your word is your word. If you said you would do something, or committed to something, you had to do that. My poor dad. One summer holiday he said he'd take us to a fishing tournament held at one of the local dams. A weather front had come down from the Congo and we were having torrential rain. It would be stupid to go fishing, but we were adamant, 'Dad, your word is your word.' We went fishing and it was the most miserable day in the rain. We didn't catch a fish and I can't remember anyone else catching one either. Mum usually came on all our adventures. She had grown up with an adventurous brother and she loved getting involved and watching us boys have fun. But on this occasion she was happy to let us head off by ourselves, returning home drenched, hungry and cold later that evening.

Sport was compulsory at Midlands Christian School. We all played rugby, cricket, hockey and did the compulsory athletics and cross-country. By the time Steve started at school, Mike and I were doing sport (which started in Grade 3) so he just joined in instead of waiting around with my mum, who would take us home. He even ran in the school cross-country day when he was in pre-primary and did well compared with a lot of the eight-year-olds in Year 3. He was always incredibly tough, probably because of growing up with two older brothers.

Dad coached the Midlands Christian College First XV, so, after we finished our rugby training at 3.30PM, we would hang around, passing the ball on the sideline, helping put the hit shields out, practising our kicking and trying our best to get involved in the training session in some way. My dad has a real gift for working with young men, and the results he got with his rugby team were great. He always seemed to get the tough, off-the-rails, nothing-but-trouble kids to play and used rugby as a way to spend more time with them and help them work on other parts of their lives. I know many of the young people he taught and coached still stay in contact with him. If I meet them on my travels, their faces light up as they tell me stories of Dad at school and how much fun they had.

I remember my mum and dad once organised a Form 2 (Grade 9) camp at my grandfather's game farm with about sixty kids all camping. For one of the team-building activities Dad had organised rope crossings over a river that ran through the property. It was hardly the most challenging rope crossing—my brothers and I didn't have too much problem getting across. The difficulty seemed to arise when the kids realised that the river had crocodiles in it. There weren't many crocs around but they were in there, and some of the students started freaking out. There was no reason to fall off, but fear is a fascinating thing. It's amazing how it can take a grip of someone's mind. I'm sure everyone was a little scared crossing that river via two ropes tied to trees on either bank. But what made some people get across without a problem, what made them act in spite of fear? And what caused other people to be totally paralysed by this fear? The thought of it overwhelmed them. A few people panicked halfway across and fell in, and my brothers and I were in a kayak to help rescue them. But you try, as an eight-year-old, to get a panic-stricken teenager, who believes he's going to be pulled under (albeit in waist-deep water) and death-rolled any minute by a monster crocodile, into a kayak! It didn't work. They inevitably scrambled their way to the closest bank, clawing at the water at an almost unbelievable rate—to squeals of laughter from me and my brothers. But Dad has a knack for helping people overcome their fears and by the end of it everyone had crossed via the rope—and I mean everyone. The sense of achievement among the group was amazing.

When things were going better on the farm, Dad moved back from teaching to full-time farming and when I was in Year 5 he had time to coach our Colts team. My brother, Mike, played hooker. There was no one else I would rather have at the middle of the scrum. He was tough and when he got angry—well, that's when things got fun. I remember he lost it once or twice on the rugby field—he never did anything illegal—but woe to any opponent who pushed him too far. On one occasion a boy on the opposite team was taunting him, calling him names. The next time that kid carried the ball, Mike shot out of the line and put on a huge tackle, the ball spilt forward and the ref blew his whistle. I gave him a brotherly pat on the shoulder as the other kid lay on the ground whimpering, no doubt regretting the name-calling.

I had played Colts (Under-10s) when I was in Grade 3 and 4 so when I was in Grade 5 I was really excited about not playing up, about actually playing with my classmates. But after the first tournament of the season there were complaints from some of the other schools, and the headmaster decided I was to play in the Under-12s. So I went from playing No. 10 for the Under-10s—straight onto the flank for the Under-12s the next weekend. It would prove to be a somewhat similar switch in position at the end of high school.

All through primary school I did most of the kicking. I had a really good kick for a kid my age, mostly because I used to practise so much on the farm and prided myself on my drop kicks.

After playing for the Under-12s in Grade 5 and 6, Grade 7 was a very exciting year. My age group was pretty strong and we had a really handy team, coached by my dad and Simon Gough—he was my Grade 5 teacher, such a fantastic man who was very passionate about rugby and also about having fun, something that we did as a team. That year we played twenty-eight games, lost one, drew three and won the rest. Largely due to my mum's amazing organisational skills and a lot of fundraising, we even managed to tour the Eastern Cape of South Africa, playing five games with four wins and one loss—our only loss the entire year.

Looking back, Midlands Christian School (MCS) is where I got my love of rugby and love of the team environment, where you are playing with your mates and being challenged, and winning. I have always hated losing. I found losing almost unbearable. I would replay the game over and over in my head, working out what I could have done better, and what I needed to work on to improve and help the team win. Dad played such a big role in my rugby early on and Mum has always been so supportive and has devoted so much of her time to my brothers and I, our schooling and our sport.

Simon Gough also played a big role as a mentor at MCS. He was someone I really looked up to, who affirmed that it was ok to be a boy who was boisterous and enjoyed fun, made mistakes and got his uniform dirty—it was all just part of it. Two things that were not negotiable with Dad and Simon were sportsmanship and respect for the referee. I am glad they put so much emphasis on these. At the end of the day sport is to be enjoyed and there is no sport without referees.

I played in the Zimbabwe primary schools tournament in grades 5, 6 and 7 for Midlands, the small province of which Gweru is the capital. We had a tiny talent pool compared with the bigger provinces that included cities like Harare and Bulawayo. The tournaments were big events held over three days or so and a lot of fun. One of my favourite rugby moments, to this day, is playing against my cousin Tyler. Tyler was my best friend growing up, despite him and his family living in Bulawayo, a two-hour drive from Gweru, and I looked up to him as a sort of hero. He was also one of the best schoolboy rugby players I have ever seen and was feared by everyone on our team. They piled a huge score on us, with Tyler captaining Matabeleland to win the tournament. It had always been one of my goals to play a game of rugby on the same team as Tyler. It hasn't happened yet, but maybe Golden Oldies one day?

We always used to talk about the Camel Trophy, often referred to as the '4 × 4 Olympics'—it was a gruelling adventure race over challenging terrain in Land Rovers. We both loved to watch it on TV and would often try and re-enact scenarios in my grandfather's old World War II Willys jeep on his farm—taking the roads we knew were bogged during the rains, or just tracks that were seldom used, and then washing the jeep at the citrus-packing shed on our way back to the house to destroy evidence of any off-road escapades. We still talk about doing an adventure race together one day—it's just a matter of finding the time and actually qualifying for a race, I guess. It would be a lot of fun.

After finishing primary school at Midlands Christian School, I played one season of rugby at Midlands Christian College but to be honest I remember very little about it, apart from being asked by the seniors (eighteen-year-olds) to play with them in their inter-house rugby competiton (but Dad not allowing me to) and the fact that I had definitely started noticing the girls. Being a co-ed school they often watched our games on a Saturday. After our game we would all go and support their hockey games. It was compulsory for the whole school to watch the First XV and First XI hockey, so it wasn't as if we were especially eager to watch the earlier games, it was just filling time till the First team games later in the day. Well, that was the story anyway.

By the time Rugby World Cup 1999 came around, my interest in the international game had grown a lot. I was hopeful of the Springboks going all the way again in that tournament and making it a back-to-back win. The 1995 tournament was fresh in my memory—the final with the plane flying low over Ellis Park, Mandela in Francois Pienaar's No. 6 jersey, and my favourite part probably being P. J. Powers and Ladysmith Black Mambazo singing 'World in Union' in front of a packed Ellis Park. It sent shivers down my spine. Surely the Springboks could do it again in 1999?

But it wasn't to be. After the semi-final I quietly slipped out of the TV room and headed down to my bedroom to have a bit of a cry after Stephen Larkham slotted *that* drop goal in extra time for Australia to win and eliminate South Africa from the tournament. I was eleven years old.

Despite supporting the Springboks, I really liked the way the Aussies played the game and Stephen Larkham was someone I loved to hate. At the time, I was playing a bit of fly-half at school. I loved watching how effortlessly he seemed to cut through defences or throw that pinpoint pass to one of his centres to slice through untouched. I admired him a great deal, so while I was disappointed the Springboks were out of the World Cup, it softened the blow that he had kicked the drop-goal and Australia went on to win the tournament. At the time I could never have dreamed that I would one day meet Larkham while still at school, play against him in the Super 14, or then have a drink with him after I debuted for Australia in Hong Kong … never in my wildest dreams.

# 2.

# No Longer Welcome
## Time to flee our 'homeland'

I have sometimes been asked how I went from being such an ardent Springbok supporter—growing up watching them, hearing from my dad how Danie Gerber was the best centre he had ever seen, and whenever we were at farmers' meetings or *braais*, the kids played 'touch' rugby while the parents were socialising, re-enacting Bob Skinstad's dummy (and then his massive dive) to score against the Wallabies—to supporting the Wallabies and hoping to play for them.

I think this change in allegiance was largely due to the way we left Zimbabwe. After the government announced the land redistribution program, farmers in our area started receiving notices to vacate their farms. I remember going into my parents' room one night; they had a map open on their bed and Mum was reading up on Australia. I looked at the map of this massive island with another small island to its south-east. It seemed so foreign—it was just a picture on a map, a huge island with a big desert in the middle. It was home to the Wallabies and I knew them well—I had a picture of George Smith on my wall with 'Enemy Threat' written on it, which I'd taken out of a South African rugby magazine. It was a place that a few of our friends had moved to in the past few years and it was also where Crocodile Dundee and Skippy the bush kangaroo lived, but that was the extent of my knowledge of Australia.

Mum and Dad had decided we should leave Zimbabwe. This was not an easy decision and one that my parents made largely for my brothers and me. Our families had been in southern Africa for a few generations, and Mum and Dad had worked incredibly hard to build the farm up to what it was—the prospect of losing it all and moving to the other side of the world was daunting.

My great-grandfather, on my mum's side, apparently much to his family's disgust, joined the 70th Company of the Royal Imperial Scottish Yeomanry of Sharpshooters and was shipped out to South Africa to fight in the Boer War from 1900 to 1901. They landed at Beira, Mozambique, and travelled through Fort Victoria and Fort Tuli to advance on Pietersburg. He ended up being a British guard at a concentration camp in Bloemfontein in the Orange Free State. Being a guard in the concentration camp, where Afrikaner women and children were held in squalid conditions by the British, had a profound effect on him and made him very anti-British. He never returned to Scotland.

He was tremendously impressed with the Boer women and children and disgusted by the appalling conditions in the camps. There was a lack of basic sanitation, which resulted in the children dying like flies from enteric fever, which he also contracted and suffered from for the rest of his life. He said the war was a crime and was ashamed to have been a part of it. He was only eighteen when he joined up.

He later played rugby for the Ramblers Club in Bloemfontein and for the Orange Free State (today the Cheetahs) against the British touring side in 1903, in a game they lost 17–16, much to his disgust.

On the other side of my mum's family, my nana's family were originally from Alsace-Lorraine in France. They moved to Germany and then during the Huguenot revolt in the 1800s they moved to Holland. Finally, they fled Holland in an old sailing ship that was on the way to Australia. But they apparently got tired of all the water and disembarked in Cape Town.

My dad's great-grandfather, Thomas Pocock, arrived in southern Africa in the late 1800s, a missionary en route to China. The ship he was on was shipwrecked on the south-west coast—ominously called the Skeleton Coast because it caused so many shipwrecks and deaths. Thomas and the other survivors lived on penguins and penguin eggs. He eventually got to Cape Town and began his life in South Africa.

In 1960, my dad's parents left South Africa and moved to Rhodesia (now Zimbabwe). They started farming in 1969 after a few mining ventures, then sold that farm and bought a different one in the newly independent Zimbabwe in 1985. This was where I grew up. Before my grandfather died, he and his two sons, Andy and John, set up a company and ran two neighbouring farms—crops and cattle on one and dairy on the other. My grandfather died when I was two and my mum and dad continued farming, taking on the crops and cattle while my Uncle John and Auntie Debbie ran a dairy farm next door. Initially our farm produced vegetables, mainly onions, tomatoes and potatoes, as well as about eighty hectares of maize (corn), with the capacity to also run about four hundred cattle. We later had about twelve hectares of export flowers. However, despite my family being in Africa for so long, the president of Zimbabwe, Robert Mugabe, had now decided that he wanted white farmers out, which was why my family was now deciding to leave.

At the time, I didn't understand many of the reasons behind what was going on. We heard our parents talk to our neighbours and their friends about why things were happening—the economy, the army, and politics. But you pick up on feelings and emotions more than specific facts as a kid. We knew life had changed because fear began to creep into our day-to-day lives. Our parents were stressed. The farm workers were edgy and would sometimes disappear, returning with black eyes and bruises. There were hushed conversations in kitchens and bedrooms behind closed doors. There were questions we knew not to ask. The occasional gunfire would ring out at night and Dad would explain it as poachers or kids having fun, but we could sense the tension in the air. Now, as an adult, and with the blessing of hindsight and hard information, it's easy to explain these things. But at the time it just seemed like our country, our community, our lives were slowly being torn apart.

From 1965 to 1979, the white minority government in Rhodesia, led by Ian Smith, was classified as an 'unrecognised state'. This was because Britain refused to give it independence (it was part of the British Commonwealth) until there was a majority government—in other words, one that included black people. There were a number of trade sanctions set in place by the international community and a vocal independence movement led by Robert Mugabe and Joshua Nkomo.

Mugabe was elected prime minister in 1980. It didn't take long for things to start going wrong. Mugabe unleashed an army against his main rival, Nkomo and his power base, and there were massacres in Nkomo's homeland. After an uneasy truce, Mugabe turned his attentions on white Zimbabweans.

Zimbabwe showed the first signs of things to come in late 1997 when Mugabe paid billions of dollars of unbudgeted funds to war veterans after their funds had all but disappeared, due to party corruption. This was the start of the now-famous demise of the Zimbabwean dollar. In 1998, Mugabe sent troops to back government soldiers in the conflict in the Democratic Republic of Congo and this placed enormous strain on the already spluttering economy.

In 2000, as part of a scheme of land reform, Mugabe proposed a referendum on a new constitution that would give the government the power to seize farms owned by white farmers, without compensation, and transfer them to black farm owners. After the newly formed Movement for Democratic Change (MDC) rallied enough support to defeat the proposed new constitution, Mugabe was furious. War veterans, led by Chenjerai 'Hitler' Hunzvi, and other supporters of Mugabe's Zimbabwe African Nation Union–Patriotic Front (ZANU-PF) decided that they would take back the land anyway and began occupying farms and intimidating farmers and farm workers. The government seized the opportunity to gain popularity with the black majority and implemented the proposed land redistribution anyway, while doing nothing to stop the farm invasions. Few independent observers would argue with land redistribution, but this was farcical. Mugabe's policy had little to do with equitable redistribution and, was instead, all to do with power. Government approval and lack of police intervention in the invasions became the catalyst for widespread violence, targeted at many farm workers and commercial farm owners. Hundreds of farm workers, black and white, were killed and a number of white farmers too. Land was mainly given to government ministers, party faithfuls and other supporters of Mugabe's regime.

Among the madness, there were some genuine black farmers who received land and tried to work it, but amid the failing economy, fuel shortages and a lack of seed and fertiliser supplies the majority of those efforts were in vain. It was a land of turmoil. I remember the food riots in Gweru in 2000, when people had become so desperate that they rioted and looted, stoning cars and generally causing havoc before the police fired tear gas and dispersed them. When parents arrived at school later that day to pick up their kids, cars had smashed windows and some parents had cuts and wounds that needed to be bandaged.

Our visa applications were posted to the Australian Embassy in January 2000, but by September 2001 we still hadn't heard anything. Things in Lower Gweru where we farmed started to deteriorate politically and there was a lot of fear among the farm workers and farmers.

We had also received government notices to vacate our farm. First came the 'Section 5', which basically stated that the government planned to acquire our farm for redistribution. Next came the

'Section 8', which was hand-delivered and gave ninety days notice to farm owners and workers to vacate the premises. Inventories of all irrigation, farming implements and equipment—including tractors, ploughs, diesel tanks and motorcycles—were noted. A stocktake of all stored grains and crops on the farm was also taken and all this had to be left at the farm as is: the crops would be harvested and sold by the new land owners and the irrigation systems (pumps, pipes, etc) would, in most cases, be left or sold in town. We had four hectares of flowers under lights, which had only been installed a few seasons before and were worth US$200,000. All those lights had to be left for the 'landless people of Zimbabwe' to whom President Mugabe was giving our farm.

In our case, it just so happened to be the Governor of Masvingo Province. Our farm became his weekend retreat and he never even moved onto the property. Before we left the farm, there were a few herds of zebra roaming the area. One of the herds was particularly tame, and it was cruelly slaughtered by Mugabe's supporters with automatic rifles and the meat left to rot, as if to send a message to dad: 'We will do what we want and you can't do anything to stop us.' There was no point informing the police—they refused to get involved in any 'political' matters. My father was devastated. It was just another indictment of the government's land reform program—the motives were never pure and the main beneficiaries of the land grab were Mugabe's henchmen. The average Zimbabwean profited not at all, while one million farm workers—the women and men who actually had the skills to farm the land—were displaced.

Farming was becoming near impossible, with constant harassment, workers being continually intimidated and beaten up and items, like diesel, becoming increasingly harder to get hold of. The farm workers would be beaten up and the same thing happened to many of the white farmers in the area, many of whom were beaten quite severely.

If farm workers didn't attend ZANU-PF 'crusades' (compulsory rallies) in the area, held at a school eight kilometres from our house, Mugabe's youths would come looking for them. People found not attending would be beaten and left bruised, bleeding and frequently in need of medical attention, which they generally did not receive.

After one of these rallies, when many of the workers chose not to go because they wanted nothing to do with ZANU-PF and they wanted to protest against the abuse that they had been enduring for the past few years, war veterans with their youth militia arrived to dish out the punishment for not attending the compulsory rally. Facing the prospect of severe and ongoing beatings, the farm workers said that my dad had told them that they had to work and couldn't attend. This is totally understandable—these people had been terrorised for months and had families to care for. So the thugs decided that my father, Andy, would be the next white farmer to be made an example of and 'taken out'.

By this stage, all the outside communication we had was via the radio because electricity and phone lines were not working a lot of the time. Phanuel, our farm foreman—an amazing man who I really looked up to—radioed my dad to tell him not to come back from town one day because there were two men, both of whom were armed—one with an AK-47 and the other with a pistol—'waiting to shoot him'. Being the stubborn farmer he was and deciding that if he didn't go out to the farm that day they would probably just come back the next, he decided to try and sort it out. Ignoring the advice, he drove out to the farm and was greeted at the flower-packing shed by the two men who had been waiting for him. They had been sent by the war veterans to 'deal with him'. He went over and greeted them, and managed to talk and reason with them, and somehow turn it around. Eventually he ended up sending the men, with their AK-47 and pistol, on a grand tour of the farm with Phanuel to try and appease them.

This seemed to do the trick and, once they had helped themselves to some produce from the vegetable garden and left, Phanuel told my dad: 'Surely today your god was with you, because those men said that they were glad that they talked to you before they shot, because you are a good *mukiwa* [white man].'

Things were becoming tenser in the country. A farmer about fifteen kilometres from us was strangled with barbed wire and his house burnt on top of his body. Another farmer and his son, who lived in our area, were ambushed one night as they went back to their property and found one of their gates closed. Ian, the son, got out to open it and automatic rifle fire began. His father, Henry, was killed but Ian somehow managed to survive, despite taking nine bullets and being left for dead. My dad had a very close relationship with Ian. When things had been tough on the farm, Dad had taken a job at our high school, Midlands Christian College in town, teaching agriculture, coaching the First XV and being the sports master. It was there that he had come to know Ian.

I remember being hugely affected by this event. I was at a cricket tournament in Harare when Ian was rushed up to hospital there and, of course, we went to visit him. I will never forget looking at the bullet-ridden *bakkie* (ute) they were driving when they were ambushed—I had never seen anything like it. It haunted me even more because only a few weeks before this happened, Henry and Ian had popped in for tea to chat with my dad on our farm. Word from workers in the area was that it was Zimbabwe Army personnel who had ambushed them with fully automatic weapons.

Mum and Dad were stressed out. Steve, my youngest brother, was having serious separation anxiety issues when he was faced with the prospect of being away from my parents and there were a few nights we all slept in Mum and Dad's room. On one occasion we just had to flee the farm after being tipped off that there was a group of militia heading our way. Dad was still trying to farm but it just wasn't working. It was becoming harder and harder to be a white farmer in Zimbabwe but we'd still heard nothing from the Australian embassy. My dad wrote them a letter about our application and whether there was a possibility of speeding the process up as it had been almost a year. At this rate he didn't think we would make it to Australia, even if our family eventually got accepted under the skilled immigrant visa. We got a letter back saying that our application was in a queue and there was nothing that could be done.

By then my parents decided it was too risky to keep living on the farm. So we packed up our belongings, sent most of them to auction in town and moved into a little flat that the school leased us—Mum and Dad in one room, my brothers bunking in another and me in a caravan out the back, which suited me perfectly. There was never a shortage of games of touch rugby or basketball as the boarding houses were just a few hundred metres away. It was the perfect distraction from the backdrop of political, social and economic turmoil our country and our family was facing.

It was the first time I had ever lived in a town, albeit a fairly small one, and the noise of cars was something to get used to. Every time you heard one you thought someone was coming to visit. Our farm was about thirty kilometres outside of Gweru, which has a population of about 150,000—making it the third largest city in Zimbabwe. Gweru is situated in one of Zimbabwe's finest cattle-rearing areas. The surrounding agricultural activity revolves around the cattle industry (both beef and dairy), although flowers are also grown in the area for the export market. My parents had moved from cash crops such as tomatoes and onions to flower production as the Zimbabwe dollar continued its freefall—inflation eventually reached 231,000,000 per cent before the Zimbabwe dollar was finally scrapped in 2009.

We had the opportunity to leave, but this was not the case for the hundred or so farm workers. Some one thousand people, including all their families, didn't have the same options and were all displaced—left to go wherever they could, to try and get work and to find somewhere to live. You'd think these were the people who should be given land—people with the skills to farm it—but farm workers were very low down on President Mugabe's list of people to help and they were often targeted for intimidation and brutal beatings for 'aligning themselves with the whites'.

Many, now unemployed, farm workers headed for the South African border, along with thousands of other Zimbabweans seeking employment so they could send money back to their families in Zimbabwe. By 2007, this mass immigration had turned into what was dubbed by the South African media as 'the human tsunami' of illegal immigrants. Thousands of Zimbabweans crossed the crocodile-infested Limpopo River every day. At the last Zimbabwe census, just prior to the 2000 elections, police sources estimated that six to ten thousand undocumented migrants were crossing the border a week. Zimbabwe's population was estimated at eleven million in 2000, but by the end of 2007 this was down to seven million.

After moving to town, my parents considered applying for refugee status in Canada. But the Canadian government wouldn't even grant us a holiday visa because they said we were too high a risk of being overstayers due to the situation in Zimbabwe. While we had enough points to get into Australia as skilled immigrants, we just couldn't wait for the bureaucrats to do whatever they do. It was now nearly impossible to make a living from the land and my parents decided it wasn't worth the risk, so we headed south of the border to my grandfather's holiday house in Port Alfred on the eastern cape of South Africa. We were really just there waiting for our visas, ready to leave for our new life in Australia. We ended up being there for eight months. We received our permanent residency from Australia in July 2002 and immigrated in September of that year.

I had spent the first few months in South Africa bitter and angry about what had happened in Zimbabwe and the many lives that had been ruined. I worried about the workers on our farm, amazing people, many of whom I knew well. But that time in Port Alfred proved to be a great period for myself and my journey. I made some great friends. Mum and Dad got jobs teaching at the local high school, Port Alfred High, which I also attended. We had spent many Decembers in Port Alfred, so it didn't feel like a new place. Many of the 'new' friends I made were kids I had played touch rugby with on the beach in the past but had never got to know properly.

It was such a novelty living by the beach. I loved it—coming from a landlocked country it felt like the ocean was alive. Despite being in limbo between Zimbabwe and Australia, I had some great times, particularly involving sport—swimming, athletics, rugby and the absolute highlight, the epic touch rugby games on the beach. I made great friends and the community was really welcoming to us—a good distraction after leaving Zimbabwe and the struggles of the people still living there. I even bought a mobile phone and would wait eagerly for the text on weekends or holidays, 'Touch rugby, Kelly's Beach, low tide—3PM' and I'd be off, rugby ball in hand, to the beach. I was now on the 'locals' team during the holidays, taking on all the city slickers from Johannesburg and other big cities.

It was a time that gave me energy. I had a bit of a social life, I could walk to the beach and there were a lot of pretty girls at school— not that I was really brave enough to talk to them. The turmoil of Zimbabwe felt a million miles away, for me anyway. I know that my parents were anxious about still not hearing back from the Australian Embassy and my brothers were struggling to come to grips with all that had happened in the past year.

Steve was continuing to deal with separation anxiety and this was really tough on him. Mike was getting on with things as usual but was really missing his friends from Zimbabwe. Luckily the beach, and surfing in particular, was an escape for all three of us. Steve and I bought dodgy old surfboards and Mike had a boogie board and we were down at the water most days after school. Mum would drive past the beach on the way to pick us up from school, boards in the car, and she'd deliver her 'surf report'. If it was good we were straight there for the afternoon. Mum loved the beach probably more than all of us put together, so she spent hours sitting there reading and even jumped off the end of the pier a few times to swim out to where we were surfing, which was quite something as the break was a good seventy metres from the beach.

This time was breathing space. It allowed me to dream a bit, to think more about one day playing rugby (by this stage I was hoping to play for the Wallabies) and what that might involve and how hard I might need to work to get there. I had a job down at one of the cafes cleaning tables on weekends and that was enough to buy the odd t-shirt or some wax for my board. I never really got any good at surfing but it was just such a novelty because we were living at the beach. It was a simple life. But I had to grow up. All that I associated with my childhood was gone and I felt like I was becoming a man. The move to a new country didn't daunt me—instead I found it energising. I spent a lot of time down at the rocks on one particular beach, trying to catch fish on my hand line, but more just breathing in that ocean air and hearing those sets of waves come rolling through. It was a much-needed time of refreshment and cleansing before confronting the real challenges of moving to a foreign country and starting a new life there.

Academic study was less of a priority and I had more fun in class than I had previously. It was a bi-lingual school, so everyone spoke English and Afrikaans, which was interesting. My Afrikaans was almost non-existent, apart from 'good morning' and 'thank-you' and maybe one or two other phrases. In Afrikaans class, where I would just sit and listen, or design traps that I could use to trap wild birds, someone put me up to saying to the teacher, in Afrikaans, that her bum looked like a pumpkin. I had no idea what I was saying but it didn't seem like it sounded too offensive. Luckily she thought it was hilarious, as did the class, and I never got into trouble. My goodbye gift from the class was a Year 1 Afrikaans book which they all signed. They had given me a spark, a renewal before the big move across the Indian Ocean. I still try and keep in contact with a few friends from Port Alfred, and often get text messages wishing me well. It's such a sweet reminder of those months of living by the sea and feeling so free in that transitory space.

# 3.
# Making Peace
## Reflections by the sea

During the transition period in Port Alfred, I had started reflecting on and learning about what was happening in Zimbabwe. It was Desmond Tutu who said that there is 'no future without forgiveness'. He is someone I really respect and I decided, as painful as it was at the time, to make a real effort to try and understand what had gone on. My parents had sheltered my brothers and me from much of what occurred and growing up as whites in Africa we had taken a lot for granted, given its colonial past and the advantage that this gave us over the rest of the population.

I knew it would be easy to be bitter about my experience and blame Mugabe for all the pain. But he had done nothing to me personally and I didn't want to carry those feelings with me all my life. That'd be a painful way to live and was nothing like Jesus's advice, 'love your enemies, pray for those who persecute you'. Or Gandhi and his 'an eye for an eye makes the whole world blind'. It has been a slow and, at times, painful process, rehashing old memories and reading some gruesome and heartbreaking accounts of torture and murder, but I now have a more balanced insight into what occurred and why. My thinking has changed as well as my attitudes towards what happened to us and what happened in Zimbabwe.

My dad's parents bought their farm in 1985, after Zimbabwean independence, on a willing buyer-willing seller basis. In 1988, they set up a company with their two sons, my dad Andy and Uncle John, and began farming together. My grandfather died in 1990 and there was a Zimbabwean law requiring death duties to be paid—they amounted to almost 30 per cent of the farm's value in this case. My dad and uncle ended up having to sell their entire Brahman herd to pay these duties because my grandfather was the official landowner.

If land redistribution had been done in a similar fashion to the willing buyer–willing seller basis, with some sort of compensation scheme and with the black farmers who took over being given the skills and capacity to look after the land, I feel as though much of the strife that occurred would have been avoided. But this was not what happened. I left Zimbabwe loving Zimbabwe and my fellow countrypeople, yet hating Mugabe and not trusting the police, the army, the press, or anything else to do with the autocratic regime that had ruined the lives of millions of Zimbabweans.

For me and for the tens of thousands of families who have left, both black and white, leaving Zimbabwe was a tough experience. It was home and all I knew. I had always been so proud to be Zimbabwean. But in the media, which had become more and more controlled by the government, the propaganda created an environment full of resentment towards white farmers, with no dialogue or balance in the reporting. Many whites considered themselves Zimbabwean but now were not welcome. The government said that white farmers were less than Zimbabwean, that they had stolen all the land and that they were the reason why Zimbabwe was doing badly. It claimed that white farmers were siding with 'the British' to plunge Zimbabwe into economic chaos and were causing many of the problems, when, in fact, these were the result of politicians' greed and their serious mismanagement of the country. I agreed with the idea of land redistribution—it is such an important issue that needs to be resolved in Africa, and something had to be done in Zimbabwe. But the tragedy was that it was never about true land distribution—it was all about votes and appeasing people who had been promised money and land.

That is just my experience. I was born in 1988—eight years after Zimbabwe gained independence from colonial rule. Like everything in life, there is always a lot more to the story. I've had time to try to overcome my privileged white viewpoint and look at it less emotionally. I'm sure many older black Zimbabweans who had lived through and fought against colonial rule thought it absurd that African sovereignty was being demonised because of the abuse of white rights. Had the West not forgotten the history of Africa? Sure, Africa was now 'free', but it was a strange freedom where many whites and a select few blacks owned much of the land and businesses and had so much influence, while the vast majority of black people still lived in poverty. It was a so-called freedom leaving millions in poverty while wealthy whites lived in their secure homes and large farms, as vast resources were being taken offshore by the neo-colonialists—the multinational corporations that had remained after independence.

When the unrest and land redistribution began, many white farmers and churches started calling for prayers to preserve the status quo. From memory, there were large prayer rallies held at a few locations around the country. Why were those joining the prayer initiative not questioning the morality of wanting to preserve a system in which Africans would remain dispossessed and the whites unfairly empowered? The same religion that had promoted the stealing of land from blacks by the British now wanted to stop the reverse happening. I can see the absurdity of the situation now.

The writer Mashingaidze Gomo, a black Zimbabwean who had fought for independence, asked: 'If they were truly Christian, why would they be reluctant to relinquish everything taken by force, everything built by forced labour, and all positions and possessions acquired not by merit but by the colour of skin? Why were they not willing to return to Caesar what was Caesar's?'

It is not an easy thing to see history from the side of the oppressed, from the side of the people who got the raw end of the deal—they very seldom get to write history. History is usually written by the victor and when you are part of that victorious race or group of people, considering an alternative story challenges the paradigms through which you see the world. It challenges the stability of the world you live in. We should want a society that is inclusive of all peoples—not one built on fear and the protection of a privileged way of life for a certain group of people, but rather one of understanding and appreciation of differences, a celebration of race and religion and customs. If we are going to work for peace, we need to begin to see history from the position of the marginalised, the minorities, and importantly, the women, to hear their stories and work for true reconciliation, not just offer apologies.

Why did the prayer initiative not start with remorse and the confession of crimes against humanity, crimes of dispossession against people who happened to not be white? It's very easy to forget history when it favours you, but not when it has sentenced you to a life of poverty within a society and an economy set up by a colonial power. I can't imagine how hard that would be.

My wife Emma often talks about how history is largely written by men, generally from a male perspective, recording their own efforts. An important part of the feminist movement is to reclaim the history of women, to honour women and affirm their worth. The same applies to any marginalised, dispossessed or oppressed group—including many of those in African countries. How can countries move forward and become truly democratic without a process of deconstructing colonialism?

The colonising of Zimbabwe began with Cecil Rhodes in the nineteenth century. He managed to get Lobengula, the king of the

Ndebele of Matabeleland, to sign a treaty with Britain for small-scale mining in Matabeleland. The treaty effectively handed Rhodes all the Ndebele land to mine and stated that the company Rhodes headed, the British South Africa Company, could do anything it thought necessary for its operations. After finding out its true effects, Lobengula tried to renounce the treaty but Britain ignored him. Rhodes is buried in one of the most revered and spiritual places in Zimbabwe, the Matopo hills, along with other British colonialists—oppressors buried in the sacred grounds of the oppressed. You begin to see the pain of the colonised people and the oppression they carry in their collective psyche from centuries of being treated as second-class citizens. Why were the white Zimbabweans not talking of starting on a clean slate following independence? Was their reluctance driven by fear of relinquishing all the colonial loot to which they owed their affluence? Zimbabwe obviously still has many hang-ups from its past, and land was one issue that was handled in a haphazard and disastrous way.

I say all of these things knowing how hard my dad worked on the farm that his family bought, building it up from very little. I know how hard his mum and dad had worked on the farm and with local black people, even helping them set up stores and other business ventures. I also do not want to diminish how my mother's mum and dad bought an almost-uninhabitable block of land and turned it into a flourishing citrus farm and game reserve. Ownership of land in Zimbabwe is a complicated issue that I do not fully understand. But it is dangerous to only hear one side of it. That's my perspective.

There are some good things that can never be taken away from Robert Mugabe. He was instrumental in dismantling a racist system that most people would agree was unacceptable. But he cannot live off that. He has become a murdering tyrant willing to do anything to maintain power. A liberation fighter fights for the people—a dictator rules for himself and his cronies.

When Mugabe first came to power, he urged black and white people to work together to build a great new nation. In his famous independence speech in 1980, he declared his intention to rebuild Zimbabwe with everyone living in harmony:

*If you were my enemy, you are now my friend. If you hated me, you cannot avoid the love that binds me to you and you to me. It could never be a correct justification that, because the whites oppressed us yesterday when they had power, that the blacks must oppress them today because they have power ... If yesterday I fought you as an enemy, today you have become a friend and an ally with the same national interests, loyalty, rights and duties as myself.*

But three years later, *Gukurahundi* had begun. *Gukurahundi*, a word from the Shona language, refers to the first rain of summer that washes away the chaff left from the previous season. It is now used to refer to the civil war in Matabeleland in which up to 20,000 people lost their lives. The brutal 5th Brigade—a special unit trained in North Korea that answered directly to Mugabe—unleashed havoc all over the country attacking 'dissidents', basically anyone who opposed Mugabe. The torture and systematic murder of individuals, whole families and even villages stretched from 1982 to 1987. Soldiers cordoned off entire villages and either shot or tortured all the inhabitants. Or they starved the occupants to death by destroying food and preventing any more reaching the area. Mass graves have been found all over the countryside. The militia even threw many people down wells and mine shafts. The pain and suffering that was inflicted then still haunts these communities.

The Zimbabwean government gave the militia huge powers under a law passed by the old Rhodesian government in 1975. It prevented the prosecution of anyone in the armed forces, irrespective of what these forces did, as long as it was deemed to 'preserve national security'. Mugabe was now using the laws of the colonial government against his black rivals. He was intent on ruling with an iron fist and the West gave him the tick of approval, hailing him as a new-wave African leader— how things would change in less than two decades.

Following the government's implementation of the land redistribution program, land was given to small farmers but there was also an accumulation of land, sometimes multiple farms, by the elite. It was also a time of concerted repression of opposition movement supporters.

Just as they took our land, sometime in the past white people had taken the very same land from the black people who lived there. Just as I lay scared at night by the possibility of what might happen to my family, there were surely many more children like me who had had sleepless nights on that land. They would have experienced the most horrific events as white people took land and declared it theirs, burned their homes and displaced them, taking the best tracts for farming and 'generously' giving the blacks other areas that were of less agricultural value.

I don't wish to absolve the Zimbabwean government of heinous crimes against its own people, nor to place all the blame on Zimbabwe's colonial past. I simply want to give some historical context to issues that people may only have thought about from a white, western worldview. As my good friend Richard Brown likes to say, 'Few things are ever that black or white—there is a lot of grey.'

Emma talks about trying not to see these issues as only two opposing points of view but as a complex problem with many variables. Everybody needs to try and see through the eyes of their neighbours in order to have compassion and not repeat the same patterns.

The balance needed to be redressed in Zimbabwe after years of colonial rule, but violence is the wrong way. Gandhi believed that 'violence can never bring an end to violence; all it can do is provoke more violence'. The repressive colonial regime in Zimbabwe led to a violent struggle for freedom by oppressed blacks, but once they attained that freedom the violence never stopped, the targets have simply changed.

Surely the only way forward is the way of heroes like Desmond Tutu, who advocate reconciliation? Not a reconciliation that simply forgives and forgets, but a reconciliation that rights wrongs and allows all parties to begin sharing a common ground, realising their common humanity and making reparations for past damages. Tutu often talks about the African understanding of something called *Ubuntu*: '*Ubuntu* is the essence of being human. *Ubuntu* speaks particularly about the fact that you can't exist as a human being in isolation. It speaks about our interconnectedness. You can't be human all by yourself. A person is a person through other persons.'

If we can look past all the prejudices taught to us as we grow up and see the common ground, the simple humanity of the people around us—especially those people who do us harm—we no doubt grow as people and create a better world. When we look to alternatives to violent retributions and seek dialogue rather than conflict, we are on the journey of discovering this *Ubuntu*—this thing that binds us all together in some strange way.

I still have friends and family in Zimbabwe and have been back to visit many times. I am always amazed at the resilience and 'make-a-plan' attitude of Zimbabweans, both black and white. For all the economic and political turmoil they have gone through, it is amazing how easily people will share a laugh and continue to hope for a better future. Surely the beauty and goodness of humanity is, in some small way, winning and there is a brighter future for the country and its patient people. It is still a place very close to my heart and is a big part of my story so far. It's a part of my life that I would never change and I am extremely grateful for the opportunity to visit and help out in some small way.

# 4.
# A Fresh Start
## New life in Brisbane before a calling to the West

During the eighteen months between moving off the farm and actually landing in Brisbane, I thought so much about what life would be like in Australia. What would the country be like? What were the people like? I knew little of Australia, apart from the fact that Aboriginal people had been there for thousands of years before the British convicts arrived and other sights and sounds I'd seen at coverage of the Sydney Olympics in 2000, as well as *Skippy the Bush Kangaroo* and *Flying Doctors*, which were both broadcast on the state-owned Zimbabwe Broadcasting Corporation's only channel. I really had no idea if I'd fit in or if people would be welcoming. Would I be up-to-date academically at school? Do they learn the same stuff? What would the standard of school rugby be like? Would I be any good in comparison? Would I one day have a funny Aussie accent?

By the start of 2002 I had started to support the Wallabies. So by the time we landed in Sydney and caught a connecting flight to Brisbane I was, in my mind, on my way to becoming an Australian and had no doubt that my rugby goal was now to play for the Wallabies. I was from Zimbabwe after all—not South Africa. And, as I would soon have to explain to most Australians I would meet, no, it's not in South Africa. It is a whole separate country made up of different ethnic groups and tribes, with a different currency (well, it did at the time). There is a

51

border and everything, including a big fence, and where there is no fence, there is a river with crocodiles in it—big ones.

My dad and one of his best friends, Stefan Le Roux, who was almost part of the family when I grew up because he lived in the granny flat next to our house on the farm, had flown over to Australia in 2001. Upon arriving they hired a little campervan and drove the east coast. While they were in Brisbane they stayed at the Palace Backpackers on the corner of Edward and Ann streets. Dad had a particularly sleepless few nights there due to the rowdiness of people in the adjacent rooms, so it's a standing joke between us when he drops me off in Brisbane at the hotels we stay at when in town with the Western Force or Wallabies (which are just up the road from the backpackers). We inevitably talk about Dad and Stefan on that trip trying to decide where our family should make a fresh start.

After visiting a lot of cities and towns along the east coast, as well as visiting a few schools, he came back to Zimbabwe and said we were moving to Brisbane and that he had put us on a waiting list at a school there—Anglican Church Grammar School. At the time it meant very little to me. All I knew was that it was an all-boys school that did well in rugby and had won the rugby and rowing premierships the year Dad visited. That excited me, but at the time I had no idea how it would shape my first few years of life in Australia, nor how it would ultimately help me achieve many of my goals in rugby. The school website wouldn't even load on our internet, it was too slow (although that wasn't saying much, I can honestly not remember our computer doing anything other than struggling to send and receive emails).

We were picked up from Brisbane airport by friends from Zimbabwe, who had moved there years earlier. They were very good to us and we stayed with them for the first couple of weeks while Mum and Dad looked for a place to rent. We played cricket in the yard with their four boys, who we had played with on their farm, which was about fifteen kilometres from ours in Zimbabwe. It was great to have at least some familiar faces around as we came to grips with this new place that was so different to anywhere we had been before.

We were only in Australia a few weeks when the fourth school term started. We were straight into it and it proved to be fairly tough and quite a culture shock. My brothers and I found it hard to adjust to the size of the school. Anglican Church Grammar School or 'Churchie', as it's more affectionately known, has fourteen hundred boys in the middle and senior school. The schools we were at before then had three to four hundred people in total. Now my year group was 250 boys. Everyone talked funny too, but I must have sounded equally funny to my new classmates because they always wanted to hear my accent, asking me to 'say something'.

There was no mistaking that I was different and didn't quite belong yet, but most of the boys were friendly and it wasn't long till I started making friends. The fourth term flew past and then we were faced with the holidays. We couldn't believe how long the school summer holidays were—almost two months. Back in Zimbabwe we had three terms with three longer holidays, rather than the big summer holiday with shorter breaks between terms. It was very daunting having all this time and no real friends yet because there was no farm to play on and Dad had to work a lot. Steve's post-traumatic stress disorder (as it had been formally diagnosed) began to get a lot worse and this tormented him and placed a strain on our family as he tried to deal with it. He spent a year as an outpatient in hospital in Brisbane.

Not really knowing anyone in Brisbane and without having a whole heap to do, I joined up at the local library and took out books on strength and conditioning and followed programs on speed and strength, doing whatever I could in the local park. In hindsight I didn't give myself much of a holiday, training almost every day, including Christmas. I'd go down to the field and do sprints and fitness, some plyometrics—

jumping up onto rails or park benches—and then at night I did core, mainly just endless crunches on my bedroom floor, music blaring, followed by a stretch.

Our family settled in Carindale, a southern suburb of Brisbane, and my first game of rugby in Australia was in the Under-15 pre-season competition for Easts' Tigers Rugby Club. It was playing with the Tigers that I first met Quade Cooper—a wiry little kid with tight ringlet curls down to his shoulders who never seemed to take his cap off. As a warm-up to our first club training session, we played touch rugby and Quade embarrassed half the team, leaping and bounding with his repertoire of steps, then flicking a ball out the back. I was astounded at his skill and the unpredictability of his step. It seems little has changed in his approach, but we have both come a long way since then.

In 2002, one of the guys in my year, Morgan Clarke, invited me to a surf life-saving competition. Not having made many particularly close friends and always being keen for a physical challenge, I immediately accepted. Morgan had been Australian champion in the flags, but it was my first taste of surf life-saving and I really enjoyed it. I had a good time, although I was not expecting the ferocity of the surf swim with your legs being pulled and plenty of elbows flying as swimmers tried to get through, and stop others getting through, the pack. It was a great experience. After this we began to hang out more and became really good friends. With Morgs around there would always be laughter. Some of the teachers at school warned Mum and Dad that he wasn't necessarily the best friend for me to have. I think they were worried that he'd be a bad influence (he was known for pulling some pretty outlandish stunts and just being generally hilarious if you were a student, disruptive if you were a teacher). Mum and Dad could see how good our friendship was for me—it provided me with the kind of fun that teenage boys are supposed to have, and which I'd been missing since moving to Australia. Ironically, Morgan is one of the most naturally intelligent people you'll ever meet and aces whatever he does with seemingly very little study. Since school, Morgan and I have remained great friends. We climbed Mount Kilimanjaro together and visited Zimbabwe, and I visited Morgan in South America a few years ago when he was there on exchange.

Morgs and I ended up sitting next to each other in a lot of the classes we were in together. Chemistry was always a highlight. Morgan was in our experiment group and we adopted a very hodge-podge approach to experiments—if the instructions were one gram of hydrochloric acid, we would put in five grams. Our results were never the intended ones but always more spectacular. Afterwards we would work backwards mathematically, to try to get the results we should have, had we followed instructions, so it didn't impact on our marks. One incident involved making chlorine gas that we were supposed to take a quick smell of, but Morgs inhaled more than his fair share and ended up very hazy, lying flat on the floor. Luckily the teacher was helping another group and we managed to pull him back up and prop him against a desk long enough to avoid the teacher finding out about it.

By 2003, I was hell-bent on making the Under-15A team in rugby. I was fifteen years old and it was the start of issues I had with my body image and my need for control over what I ate, how much I trained and many of the almost obsessive habits I developed. I did core exercises every night, without fail. I had to do them, I couldn't sleep without doing them. If I ever missed a night (due to travel or another reason) I would do double the next day. When I first started travelling with the Force, I used to sneak into the hotel gym to do the exercises or, if the gym was closed, I'd put a towel down in the bathroom. I was embarrassed about it—probably because I knew it wasn't a particularly healthy habit and that it had more to do with some sort of control over myself than physical performance on the rugby field. I did those exercises every night until the end of 2008, when I realised that it was really unhealthy and there were smarter ways to train.

I ended up playing fullback for the Under-15As in 2003. The First XV had a pretty gun team that year and went through undefeated. It was a thrill to watch someone like Karmichael Hunt tear defences to shreds with his step on Saturdays and then walk the same corridors as him during the week. Our Under-15 team was pretty decent too and we also went through the year undefeated.

My first representative honours in Australia also came in 2003 when I made the Metropolitan East team on the wing. I was pretty handy on the wing back then, nothing flash, but I got through a lot of work and ended up scoring quite a few tries, including an important one in the final. Before the game I chatted to Dad and he said that, because it was so wet, if I was going in for a try I should just dive from five or so metres out and my momentum would take me over. I got the ball on the wing with a few boys in front of me but just dove at their feet and slipped straight past, coming up covered in mud from head to toe, but scoring the try. We ended up winning the tournament. Dad was always my hero growing up. I would love asking him questions and if he ever told me anything I considered it gospel. This time was no different.

We'd been living in Brisbane for a year when Australia hosted the 2003 Rugby World Cup. This time I was supporting Australia when that intercept try by Stirling Mortlock in the semi-final inspired the Wallabies to a thrilling victory over the All Blacks in Sydney. Now 'we'—Australia—were in the final. During the pool stage of 2003, I went to watch France v Fiji and Samoa v South Africa at Suncorp Stadium in Brisbane. It was the first time I had seen international rugby live— well ... if you don't count the Sharks v Zimbabwe in Bulawayo when I was seven or eight, the Sharks beating them 100 something to very few with Springbok prop Ollie Le Roux even taking the last conversion.

I was swept up in the atmosphere of the World Cup, watching the Fijian flyer Rupeni Caucaunibuca score an amazing try against France right in front of us and then do his trademark aeroplane celebration, and that absolutely huge hit on South Africa's Derick Hougaard by 'the chiropractor', Brian Lima from Samoa.

Watching the final from our living room in 2003 I remember how Lote Tuqiri towered over Jason Robinson to score that try for Australia off a Larkham cross-field kick, but then Robinson scooting his way to the try line from a Jonny Wilkinson pass. It was such a tight game. Elton Flatley kicked incredibly well for Australia, keeping them in the game, but Jonny Wilkinson seemed to always level things up, and then *that* drop kick—the drop kick that won the World Cup for England on Australian soil. I felt pretty down about it all. Our family had only been in Australia a year but this was definitely home now and there was no other team we were supporting. It was all that was spoken about at school for the next few weeks. We were all throwing the ball around, playing touch rugby every lunch break and dissecting the game as we remembered it.

I missed almost the entire school season in Year 11 with a knee injury. I had been training really hard and was set on trying to make it into the First XV, but injured my knee in pre-season, playing club rugby for Easts at fly-half in a game that Quade wasn't able to play. I had been playing in the centres and at fullback, but without Quade I was shifted to fly-half and got hit in the air doing a clearing kick and landed awkwardly on my knee, bruising the bone and tearing the posterior cruciate ligament. It didn't seem too sinister at the time, but ended up keeping me out for much of the school season, mainly due to the bone bruising.

I was still hell-bent on playing for the First XV and had been training hard, but my family had decided that we needed a break from the city and were going to drive up to Queensland's famous Whitsunday Islands for a holiday. Mum had found a special on a yacht for hire and that was going to be our Easter break. It sounded great, but how was I going to train? It is ridiculous in hindsight, but I only agreed to go on the condition that we take some weights. We took a bench press with one hundred kilograms or so of weight. My poor family—I am so grateful that they put up with me. Weights training on a rocking boat is not ideal, but it didn't stop me, and I did what I could. More importantly, we also had a great time as a family.

My knee injury was my first encounter with a relatively serious injury and I didn't handle it well. Training and sport was how I had dealt with the move to Australia. I had become so focused on it, then it all started to unravel. I couldn't play, couldn't train as much. I couldn't understand at the time why, after all the hard work I had put in, I would get injured. I remember telling my dad that his old 'you reap what you sow' motto was no good because I trained harder than anyone in the First XV rugby squad and now look what I had reaped. He just encouraged me to use it to work on other things and that eventually all the hard work would pay off. I was painful to live with. Talking about it on a recent trip to Brisbane, my brother Mike said: 'I learnt to just leave you alone because you were always going to get your own way anyway, so what was the point in trying to argue. You were obsessed with training and what you thought you needed to do. We always used to be waiting for you to finish training in the afternoons before we went home.'

A man my dad got to know at work had heard about the trouble I was having with my knee, how much I enjoyed rugby and how I was a huge Stephen Larkham fan. I had read Larkham's 2003 *World Cup Diary* and loved watching him play. Larkham was related to Dad's work friend and when the Wallabies were in Brisbane he managed to organise for me to meet Stephen and have a quick chat with him. I was so excited as we waited in the hotel foyer in Brisbane for the Wallabies to return from training. I was really nervous too. I was meeting a legend of Australian rugby and one of my heroes.

Sure enough, as the Wallabies walked past to head up to their rooms

Stephen stopped by and sat down with me and my dad. He asked me how my rugby was going and wanted to know if I had any questions. Of course I did. I had been watching him play since we were living on the farm outside Gweru. Now I could ask him questions, I was not missing this opportunity. I asked him whether or not he consciously held his hands up to where he had passed the ball for fractionally longer than most other players. He talked about following through when you pass— hands to target. I asked about his preference for end-over-end kicks, as opposed to torpedo punts, and what to look for when practicing. He told me about trying to kick straight through the ball and avoid making the ball move off its line and return to it in flight. I hung off every word and wrote it all down when I got home.

I felt a bit embarrassed that he had taken the time to talk to me and I shyly asked if he would sign my copy of his book. He said that was not a problem and wrote in it: 'Be patient. I'm sure higher duties will come your way down the track. Regards, yours in rugby, Stephen Larkham.' I have been too shy to tell him this story the other times I have met him, but thinking back it was very generous of him to agree to talk to me, and obviously says a lot about the kind of person he is. For him it was something extra on top of his busy schedule, but for me it was an amazing experience that I was so grateful for at the time and got a huge buzz from. I remember just standing with my dad afterwards smiling—just smiling. I had just met Stephen Larkham, and I had asked him questions and he had signed his book that I had read. It was a good day.

I played for the Churchie Under-16As for the final game of the year and was lucky enough to be invited to the Queensland Under-16 trials, where, after advice from the First XV coach at Churchie, Tom Barker, I asked to be trialled as a loose forward and was selected as blindside flanker for the Queensland team at the Under-16 national championships in Sydney. Tom thought I would do well at flanker and had talked to me about the move after I'd played in the backline for the Under 15s in 2003. I had also managed to make an appearance for the First XV from the bench against Brisbane Grammar School for the last game of the season and that ended my rugby for 2004. It had not been what I had hoped for but I was confident that, if I worked hard over the summer holidays, I could play for the First XV in 2005 and hopefully make the openside flanker position my own and push for higher honours.

After the disappointment of an injury-ravaged 2004, the following year was quite the opposite and turned out to be a really big year for me. I had trained as a loose forward during the pre-season but a few weeks before the season started our First XV coach, Tom Barker, took me aside and asked whether I would play at inside centre. His reasoning was that we had quite a few flankers and had good coverage all over the field, but inside centre was one position that was a potential weakness for us. I had set my heart on playing on the side of the scrum, but was very willing to play inside centre if it meant our First XV was stronger. We had a pretty talented age group and had high hopes for the year. Towards the end of Year 12, I had been playing some good rugby for Churchie at inside centre. Quade Cooper, who'd started at Churchie by this point, was playing at fly-half. We had played together in various teams over the previous few years, from club rugby to junior rep stuff, so we were pretty familiar with each other. We had spent weeks in camps together for Queensland Under-16s and were both part of the National Talent Squad which trained most days at Ballymore before or after school, so I had got to know Quade quite well and really grew to love this kid from Tokoroa in New Zealand with his casual approach and freakish skills. I loved playing outside him and he provided a spark in our backline that saw us go through the season undefeated.

We were aware that Super Rugby talent scouts attended some of our First XV games, but few people were approached during the season. So it came as quite a surprise when I received a call midway through the school season from John Mulvihill—the newly appointed Western Force assistant coach under John Mitchell, who would lead the franchise in its inaugural year. They had seen a few of my games and wanted to know if I would consider joining the Force the following year as an 'apprentice'. There was much excitement in our family home. I could hardly believe it. I had not even played for Queensland Schoolboys, the national championships in Canberra were not for a few months, and I had already had an offer.

Mum and Dad obviously had concerns about me moving over to Perth by myself as a seventeen-year-old. But the Force offered to fly Dad and I over for a weekend to meet the two Johns (Mitchell and Mulvihill), both of whom would have a big influence on my career in the years that followed. The Queensland Reds then offered me a spot in their academy for the 2006 season. So after flying to Perth to meet the coaches and hearing what they had planned at the Force, listening to Mitchell tell me that he believed in bringing young talent through and that everyone would get some game time in the trial games, it was time to make a decision. The money from the Reds was more than double the Force offer, but the opportunity of training day-in, day-out with the professional squad in Perth was an opportunity I couldn't turn down. I rang John Mulvihill to accept the offer and work out when I would start training.

Meanwhile, I had played for the Queensland Schoolboys and had been selected for the Australian Schoolboys, which included a tour of the United Kingdom and Ireland that had us only returning back to Australia on 23 December. The Force resumed training after their Christmas break on 2 January and I would be there. I had supported the Reds since moving to Australia, but they had David Croft as their openside and he was well established and a solid player who was not going anywhere for at least a good few years. The Force was unknown, I would be training with the main squad, not in the academy, and I backed myself to learn and improve and push for a position in the team.

The Australian Schoolboys tour of the United Kingdom and Ireland was an amazing experience. We had a pretty decent team, including Quade Cooper, Kurtley Beale, James Hanson, Jack Lam and a number of guys who went on to get professional rugby contracts in Australia and overseas. It was my first time outside Australia and southern Africa and it was just so different. We were billeted out, which was a real lottery at times. But most of the billets were fantastic and it gave us such good stories, while we got to experience some of the culture and meet people who we wouldn't have met had we just stayed as a team.

My favourite story from the tour was when we were in Limerick, Ireland, and I had been billeted out with a family in a village out of town. Quite a few guys had been rested for the midweek game against Munster, as we played the Irish Schoolboys team on the weekend. Wanting to at least do some fitness training, on the way home from the game I asked my billet if he could drop me six or so kilometres from the house and I would run the rest of the way. I had been with them for a few days and was reasonably sure I would find my way to their house.

As I ran past three caravans on the side of the road—presumably belonging to Irish nomad 'pikies'—I heard a familiar snarl. When we had lived in town in Zimbabwe we had an Alsatian for security and its sinister snarl was unmistakeable. Without even thinking about it I took off—I mean I sprinted as fast as my legs could carry me. Luckily I saw the dog chase for ten metres or so and then slink back to the caravans, so I knew it was no longer chasing, but I only slowed a little. I was pretty keen by now to get back to my billet's place for dinner as it was starting to get dark. An hour later I finally admitted to myself that I was well and truly lost, so I walked up the path of a house and knocked on the door. I was greeted by a lovely Irish woman. I explained I was lost and needed to phone the people I was staying with. She knew my billet family and quickly phoned them and the father arrived five minutes later to take me back to their place. He roared with laughter as I told him the story and showed him where I had gone. I had run straight past their house without even realising it—I thought all the driveways looked fairly similar anyway—and ended up doing about eleven kilometres in total.

Some of the boys weren't as lucky as me in terms of billets—Ben McCalman was billeted out in one place with a family who all smoked. He would turn up to training smelling like smoke and for dinner was given a single piece of supermarket-bought pizza. They even had an elderly aunt, who lived with the family, offer to help him wash his back in the shower.

I had little time to spend with my family before I had to pack my suitcase again and get on a plane to Perth on 1 January. Mum was in a bit of a state at the thought of her eldest son leaving home and moving so far away, but she also knew that this was all I had wished for, my reason for training so hard through my school years in Brisbane. My obsessive training habits were hard to live with and I'm so thankful my family had been so tolerant. Now it was time to deliver on the dreams I had as a child in Zimbabwe watching Currie Cup games. Never could I have known back then that my Super Rugby calling would eventually come from Western Australia, of all places.

When I first arrived in Perth, Brett Stapleton and I stayed with a family who were connected with the Force for two weeks. Brett and I had played Australian Schoolboys together, so it was good to have a relatively familiar face within the new surrounds. The family were great and had a massive house on the Swan River. There was an option to stay for a while, but I was keen to get out, be independent and make friends. So within two weeks, I had moved out with one of the other new guys in the team—Gavin Debartolo. Gavin had been playing club rugby in Sydney, and had also been given an 'apprentice' contract, which was very little money but did have a $100 per week accommodation allowance, so we moved into a place in Scarborough for just over $200 a week.

Gavin was a good guy and had some great skills on the rugby field but I found living with him pretty funny. It's fair to say that he just loved to socialise and party. I'd get home and ask him what he was up to and he would reply, 'Just going to have a quiet night, watch some TV, and get some sleep.' Not long after I'd hear his phone beep and the next thing he was dressed up, hair done and ready to go, running out the door to be picked up by one of the boys heading out for the night: 'Just going out for a while, Bam, see you in the morning.' I used to have a good chuckle. He also had a lot of friends who were women and they sometimes came over to hang out or have dinner, which wasn't terrible. I was pretty shy and hadn't really made any friends who were girls till Year 12. By the end of Year 12 I had a girlfriend, but after a few months in Perth we decided that we were too young for a long-distance relationship and ended it. We still keep in contact and she is a great woman.

Looking back on it now, I was a somewhat boring housemate. With such limited cooking skills, I had my favourite dish and remained very faithful to it—kangaroo steak and stir-fried veggies almost every night. I was often bored with it, but it was easy to do and cheap. I was on very little money in my first year at the Force. Luckily I had sold my portion of the sheep that my brothers and I owned back in Zimbabwe, thanks to Pop who sent a few up to our farm when we were younger. They had bred up and, after Dad took a few as payment for looking after them, we each got just over US$1500 from memory, which was quite a fortune to us then. I'd also sold my motorbike for US$1000 when we left Zimbabwe and I had put it all into shares when we arrived in Australia. I was really lucky and had more than doubled my money. In Year 12 I sold all my shares, so I had a bit of cash and Mum and Dad

ABOVE: Eating sadza (a thick porridge made with corn meal) with Tshabeni out the back of our farmhouse in Zimbabwe.

BELOW: Pointing at my Dad as he takes a photo of my mum, Jane, younger brother Michael and me in front of rows of onions on the farm in 1990.

ABOVE: With my Pop at his holiday house in Port Alfred, where we eventually lived while we waited for our visas to Australia.

BELOW LEFT: Tackling during a game against Matabeleland for Midlands Province.

ABOVE: Midlands Christian School First XV of 2000.

BELOW LEFT: Winning the Victor Ladorum at our school sports day with Rugare Mudzingwa in 2001. BELOW RIGHT: Morgie and I celebrating one of his tries on our way to an undefeated premiership in 2005 with Churchie.

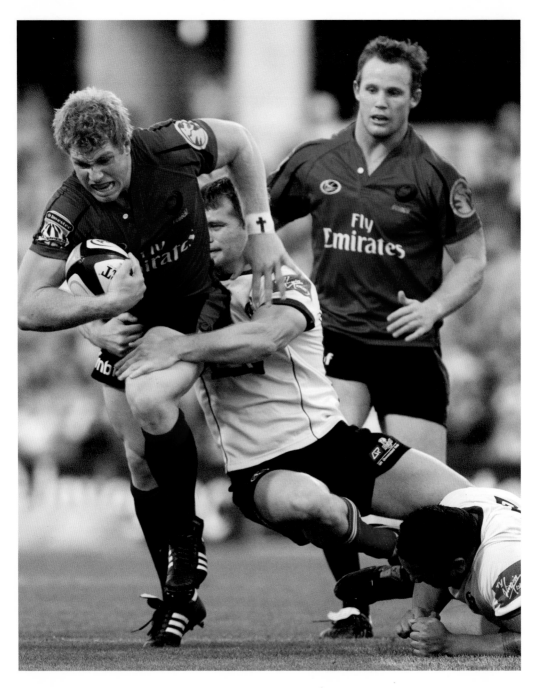

Above: Early days with the Force with Richard Brown in support.

ABOVE: Australian Schoolboys in 2005. To the left of me is Ben McCalman and James Hanson and on the far right Kurtley Beale and Quade Cooper (half in shot).

ABOVE RIGHT : High-pants Friday with Morgs on our Zimbabwe trip.

BELOW: With the 'old bull', Brendan Cannon, after we beat the Bulls at Loftus in 2007.

ABOVE: Morgs and I looking rather unimpressed on the summit of Kilimanjaro.

BELOW: Housemates at the time, Chris O'Young and I after a game for the Force.

ABOVE: Sharing a joke with Quade at the Wallaby squad announcement for the 2008 Spring Tour. From left: James O'Connor, Quade Cooper, Robbie Deans, myself and Sekope Kepu.

BELOW: James, Quade and myself in Hong Kong on our first Spring Tour in 2008.

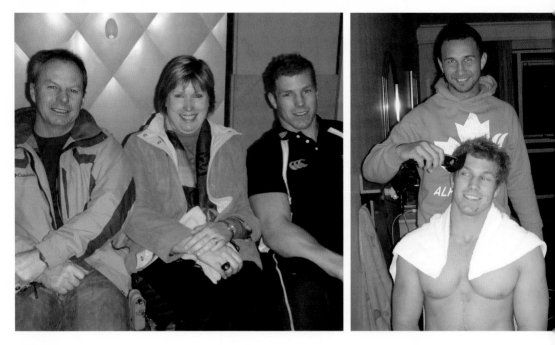

ABOVE: Dad, Mum and I in Italy as they backpacked around Europe, following the 2008 Spring Tour.

ABOVE RIGHT: Quade looking a bit too pleased about my haircut during the 2008 Under-20s World Championships in Wales.

BELOW: My first big opportunity with the Wallabies. Forty minutes in the London Olympic Centenary match against the Barbarians, Wembley Stadium, 2008.

would help out whenever I ran short at the end of the month.

If I got adventurous, I would call Mum from the supermarket to ask her about some ingredient that I'd need for a certain recipe. Sometimes I'd call to find out what a vegetable she'd put in a certain dish looked like before it was cooked. The times when Mum did come over to Perth, she would usually make up a whole lot of vegetable pies and other things and leave them in the freezer for me. I have gradually got better and now I'm very lucky as Emma is an amazing cook and has taught me a lot about food and cooking.

One of the more obscure things I did when sharing my first place in Perth was ask my manager to get me a discount on twenty-five rugby balls. I then went to a hardware store, bought some netting and made a basketball hoop-like thing which I suspended at chest height in the tiny courtyard and practiced my passing into it. The balls would go through the hoop and collect in the net. I really was a boring housemate.

I stayed with Gavin for a year in Scarborough, but then he went back to Sydney so I moved out by myself into a little place in Cottesloe in the same apartment block as Scott and Sarah Fava. It was nice to have my own space in Cottesloe, but being around a team environment by day almost trains you to live with others so I decided to share a place again, this time with Scott Daruda and Pat O'Connor for two years, then with Chris O'Young. Chris is definitely my favourite person who I've lived with and it was while there that I started to grow up and clean up more, keeping things a lot more tidy. It was not that I was a grub before—cleaning just wasn't the highest priority and when you are living with two other people it's always a grey area about whose mess it is. But when there are just two of you, if it's not his it's yours.

Before my first training session with the Force, I was nervous about meeting all of the really recognised players. My first encounter with one of the 'big dogs' did little to calm those nerves. At that first session I called Brendan Cannon by his full name during one of the drills and he turned around and said, 'Who calls me Brendan?'

From then on it was 'Canno' and a year or so later 'Old Bull'. Canno had a big influence on me when I first arrived at the Force. He had been playing for the Wallabies for a while and was well respected as a player and off the field he was also such a great bloke. He used to sit, for what seemed like hours to me, in the hot spa after training sessions. I didn't see him jump in the cold one too often, but if you were ever in the hot spa when he was there, he was genuinely interested in how you were going and what you were up to outside of rugby.

Canno gave me some really good advice as a young bloke starting out and he had a real level head on him. I was very disappointed when he was forced into early retirement with a neck injury. With his commentating gig we manage to catch up every now and then and have a chat. He's the kind of guy that I hope I can be like one day, giving younger guys advice and being a steady influence in a club. Mum recently saw Fiona Cannon, Brendan's wife, in Brisbane. Fiona was talking about how she used to joke that I was Brendan's shadow and that it's paid dividends now: their son Joey (who has a picture of Brendan and me in his room) said recently, 'Dad, I think I might like to play 7 like Poey instead of 2 like you.'

My first gym session with the team was equally memorable. I was doing some chin-ups, when Luke Doherty came up behind me and started shouting 'Bam Bam! Bam Bam!' at me. It comes from the animated TV series, *The Flintstones*, which had a toddler called Bamm-Bamm—the adopted son of Barney and Betty Rubble. Bamm-Bamm's excessive and sometimes misused strength was quite often the object of humour in the cartoon. I was the youngest at the Force at that time, and quite strong, so I guess that's how Luke came up with it. But that was it, the nickname stuck and a lot of guys still call me that today. In that sort of environment the more you protest the more things stick and I think I may have protested a little too much.

What excited me most about the move to Perth was the assurance that I would train with the senior squad. Coach John Mitchell, 'Mitch', had said to me that everyone at the Force would get game time in the trials and it wasn't long before I got my chance. I could already sense from training that it was a big step up from schoolboy rugby, with the calling structures and names for all the moves, etc. It took me a while to get my head around it. Dad flew over from Brisbane for our first trial against the Cheetahs and I spent the morning of the trial with him going over the calls and moves, I had only been there a few weeks and much of the squad had been training since October.

My first match for the Force was huge for me. Not just for the fact I would get a chance to play against the Cheetahs in front of more than 37 thousand people at Subiaco Oval, but it also said a lot about Mitch's mindset—he was always open to new players and he would back younger guys to play if he felt they were good enough. That really excited me.

I'm not too sure how many people knew about the eighteen-plus rule for Super Rugby, but as it got closer to the trial game it became an issue. Under Australian Rugby Union (ARU) regulations, I was ineligible to play because I was still only seventeen. Even after my parents signed a waiver I was still not allowed to play and eventually they played me under the name of one of the injured players in the team. It probably would have all been fine, because it was just a trial game and, unless Mitch wanted to play me in the Super Rugby season, there would have been no problems. However, *The Australian* did a story on the Force's first trial match and decided to use a picture of me in it, which alerted the ARU to the fact that I had played. It wasn't really an issue for Mitch. I had Under-19 world championships coming up and he said that I should focus on that and enjoy age-group rugby while I had a chance. There was a fair bit of media attention around it at the time  and the ARU eventually changed the rule to 'if you're good enough, you're old enough'. Since then the likes of James O'Connor and Kurtley Beale have both made their Super Rugby debuts at seventeen.

The Under-19 world championship in Dubai was a great highlight for me in 2006. We had a really good team with the Faingaa twins— Saia and Anthony— plus Will Genia, James Hanson, Sam Wykes, Ben Daley and a host of others. There was also some quality among the other sides, with Victor Vito the captain and tournament star for New Zealand, while Danny Cipriani and Dan Cole lined up for England. We lost to New Zealand in the pool stage after a charge-down try, but we enjoyed revenge over the 'Baby Blacks' in the final to claim the championship. I did well personally and was the starting No. 7, but unfortunately I picked up an ankle injury in the final, which would ultimately delay my first-ever Super Rugby cap.

Beyond the rugby field, Dubai was a real eye-opener for me. We went on a desert safari camp where we had dinner with all the teams, ate fresh dates and rode camels, which was really good fun. By day in the city you couldn't help but notice the contrast of all the money and wealth in the big buildings compared with the relative poverty of many immigrant workers and locals. It was quite a weird city to take in. I was beginning to think more and more about the sort of disparities I was seeing in places like Dubai where it exists so blatantly and between my childhood in Zimbabwe and subsequent teenage years in Australia. It was pretty jarring and left me with a lot of questions about the inequality I could see in the world.

Immediately following the Under-19 world championships in Dubai I flew directly to Johannesburg to meet the Force during their South African tour at the back end of the Super Rugby season. After I had hurt my ankle in the Under-19 final, I was unable to play in the first two games in South Africa, which included a narrow loss to the Lions and a historic first win over the Cheetahs in Kimberley. That breakthrough victory was something we really needed as a team, and with an eight-day turnaround before our final match all the boys went out on the

Saturday night in Johannesburg. I decided to stay behind at the hotel to ice my ankle, and try to speed up the recovery in the hope of being ok to play some role in our final match.

The next day was a day off and the hotel was a ghost town with everyone sleeping in or doing their own thing. I remember just sitting around all day, icing my ankle and doing what weights I could in the gym. That 'recovery' day happened to be my eighteenth birthday so it wasn't overly memorable, but what awaited me the following weekend quickly made up for any disappointment felt there.

The Sharks in Durban was our last game of the season. Mitch told me he wanted to give Matt Hodgson a rest and me a start. My first senior game of rugby (apart from the trial against the Cheetahs), running on against John Smit and his Sharks—it was finally happening. The week was a bit of a blur. I have cousins in Durban and they were at the match, which was a huge buzz for me aside from playing my first Super Rugby game. I vomited in the change room before running out. I had been so nervous all day and hadn't eaten very much at all. I couldn't eat, I just felt too nervous. I had just been part of the Under-19 world championship-winning Aussie team, but this was another story. This was professional rugby, playing with and against men I had been watching on television for a very long time.

We lost the game. I remember catching a loose ball at the back of the lineout and having a run, and Brent Russell carving us up through the centres, but apart from that I remember very little. It was John Welborn's last game of professional rugby, and my first. John is a real journeyman of Western Australian rugby—the first ever Wallaby from the state. He actually played for WA against the All Blacks when he was seventeen in 1987—the year before I was born. It was quite a contrast for each of us, and a day I'll never forget.

John was a fairly rugged lock and liked to play the game hard, so it came as little surprise to many that he was cited for some fairly serious stomping in his last outing. Despite the fact he was retiring, John still had to front a SANZAR citing commissioner and, as the story goes, he was rather controversially let off after the player he stomped, Johan Ackerman, testified to the judiciary that there was nothing to it, almost kind of winking at John who was video-linked into proceedings. John had actually spent some time playing with the Sharks in the Currie Cup, and he and Johan were good friends. Rugby is so great for that, making friendships that are life-long. I feel like I am making friendships that will last a long time.

Watching the 2007 World Cup was an altogether different experience from 2003. By that time I knew and played with a few of the Wallabies and had played against the rest of them in the Super 14, so it had a different meaning. As someone who so desperately aspired to be competing at the highest level, that was where I wanted to be. How long would it be until I would have my opportunity? George Smith and Phil Waugh had the openside flanker position sewn up, and were both performing well, so I knew it would take a lot of hard work to break into that environment. I was sure that the Wallabies would make it to the final, and then I guess anything could happen in a Rugby World Cup final.

After missing out in 2003, I thought Australia were a good chance in France. When they lost to England in the quarter-final I was as shocked as anyone and, I'm guessing like most Aussie supporters, was bombarded with texts from Kiwi friends rubbing it in. When New Zealand lost to France in their quarter-final not long after, I didn't have to send any text messages. I knew how much my Kiwi mates would be hurting, and probably regretting firing off all those group texts to their Aussie mates.

Now, four years later, to be on the cusp of participating in a Rugby World Cup was very exciting to me. To have the opportunity to be in the running, to be part of a team that has a chance to lift the Webb Ellis Cup was energising. It was motivating and there was probably no price I wouldn't be willing to pay, physically and emotionally, to be part of a team that lifted that cup at Eden Park on 23 October. We didn't make it, but that's for another part of this book.

# 5.

# Laying Foundations
## My early years in Perth amid African callings

I t was a very steep learning curve for all of us involved in the Western Force franchise during the inaugural year in 2006. The Perth community certainly embraced us well beyond expectation and it was a shame we couldn't deliver a home win. But it was pleasing to see our gradual improvement across the season. The drawn match against the Crusaders gave our loyal fans something to cheer about. It gave the squad a timely boost to morale before our road trip to South Africa late in the season, when we finally enjoyed our maiden victory against the Cheetahs. That win had been a long time coming—we'd had a one-point loss to the Stormers in Perth, a narrow loss to the Highlanders at the 'House of Pain' in Dunedin and a second draw against the Cats—so the guys really deserved the solid finish. Mitch and the coaching team had put in a lot of work on various combinations and it was a relief for us to finally see some positive results.

From a personal perspective, given my goals and expectations going into my first year of professional rugby, I had a pretty good year too. I played in the first-ever Western Force trial match (albeit a little sneakily) in front of a great crowd at Subiaco Oval, won the IRB Junior World Championship with the Australian Under-19s and made my Super Rugby debut against the Sharks in South Africa. On top of all that, I also developed some great friendships across the playing group and beyond.

Given that most of the squad had moved to Perth from the east coast or overseas, no-one had solid ties to anyone in Western Australia and the playing group spent a lot of time together. Most of us younger guys rented together and there were always group barbecue dinners and hang-outs, which produced a real family feeling. A few boys rented a place down by Trigg Beach and it was a popular hang-out spot. It was quite an old place, but a great location and was soon dubbed 'Club Trigg'. Bonfires became fairly standard during gatherings, with everyone sitting around telling stories and listening to music. Luke Doherty and Rudi Vedelago ran most of them and we'd also enjoy a good sing-along too with the iPod dock. It was a great place to chill and get to know each other.

I spent a lot of my time hanging out with Luke Holmes, and his then-girlfriend Mel. Luke bought a scooter and I bought a postie bike and we would cruise around Perth together on our days off or hang out at his place. We became really good friends and also made some other friends outside of rugby, which I found really refreshing. Luke was confident and was great at making friends, so we often had a house full of guys to chat with or play soccer or touch rugby down at the beach.

We had started talking about possibly helping out with homeless people in Perth and in an orphanage in Africa. Luke already did some work in juvenile detention centres, visiting young people in there, and we both felt there were a lot of people our age questioning how they were living and the inequalities that exist in the world, but didn't have a way to change things. We talked about getting a website to provide a place for other young people to talk about these issues and hopefully it would lead to change. We even got the website up and going and began to do a bit of work on it before Luke moved back to Sydney and then to Melbourne to join the new Melbourne Rebels franchise in 2011, where he now lives with his wife, Mel, and two sons. In the end, the idea never really got off the ground.

In 2008, on the South African leg of our Super 14 travels, Luke Holmes and I took over fifty soccer and rugby balls and handed them out at a few children's homes and then spent a day at a home in the Natal Midlands, leaving a whole heap of balls with the kids there. It was amazing to meet children who have so much joy and enthusiasm despite a tough upbringing. It was the highlight of my trip—it puts life in perspective when you're travelling the world playing rugby.

Outside of rugby, I also met Luke O'Keefe in early 2006, not long after moving to Perth. We got on well from day one. He became the person I could talk to when I was missing home or when I was feeling down, and he was eventually the friend I bounced ideas off as my beliefs began to change. We'd spend hours hanging out, usually down at the Wild Fig Cafe roughly halfway between our houses, talking about this or that. We'd discuss our views on the world, things that we were reading about—anything really. Over the years our friendship has grown and Luke and his wife, Bec, and their three boys have become my 'family' in Perth.

Luke and Bec eventually started having a group of people over on a Tuesday night to hang out and talk about how we were doing personally and spiritually and about global issues. We watched a lot of documentaries and read the odd book together. It was, in a way, a group of people who didn't think institutional 'church' met their needs yet wanted to be a part of a community in a different form. This Tuesday night group has continued and is something that I look forward to when I'm in Perth and miss when I'm away travelling.

In hindsight, I guess there was always a sense that Luke and I would eventually take on something together, to try to make some sort of difference in the world. The seed for our charity, EightyTwenty Vision, was probably sown quite early on. But, I was still relatively young at that stage—I needed to make my mark with the Force during what was shaping up as a promising second year after the high-profile signing of Matt Giteau. In what was the richest deal ever in the history of Australian rugby, the player dubbed 'Kid Dynamite' was making his way to Perth from the Brumbies and there was a lot of hype about it.

'Gits' was really well received by the playing group and fans in Perth. It was a welcome boost for team morale after having had only one victory in the first season. He was the golden child of Australian rugby and I was really excited about him and Drew Mitchell joining the team. I remember Drew's first training session with us. He is not the biggest of blokes but his footwork and balance are amazing. He impressed me so much I remember telling my dad over the phone about it later that night.

Mitch eased me into the team slowly throughout 2007 after my debut in the final match of 2006. Sometimes I would start, other times I would come off the bench, then I'd start two games and then start off the bench again. It was a gradual exposure and while I, no doubt, wanted to be starting all the time, Mitch always managed young players well. I'm thankful to have been coached by him when I was.

Our 2007 season started with another agonising one-point loss at home—to the Highlanders yet again—but we tried not to let it get us down too much. Mitch focused on getting us to work together as a group, creating a 'team culture' and habits that would serve us well, so he was usually quite positive after games. It helped a lot in our development. Thankfully, a successful two-week trip to South Africa followed, which included victories over the Stormers in Cape Town and the Bulls in Pretoria.

That win over the Bulls was fairly significant, not only for how we managed to string two victories together for the first time but for how we did it against the eventual champions on the highveld in South Africa. The main team the Bulls franchise is built around is *die Blou Bulle* (Blue Bulls), my grandfather's favourite team, so it was a little ironic for me to be celebrating an Australian win playing against one of the teams I had seen so much of while growing up in Zimbabwe.

Despite the successful tour of South Africa, the close matches continued at home and we suffered yet another one-point loss at home to the Cats. It was starting to develop into a bit of an unwanted trend with home matches, but Mitch always remained relatively positive and urged us to find solutions. As a player, it was very frustrating to continue to lose so closely but being a younger member of the playing group I was very focused on trying to work on my own game and make sure I improved. I was learning new things every game and wanted to be able to contribute more on the field and being so young and inexperienced allowed me to focus on my own game like this, as I didn't really have much responsibility or input in terms of organising the way the team played.

Our first home victory eventually came against the Hurricanes in round six of 2007 and it was a welcome relief for everyone. It didn't come easy though, with a last-minute try and conversion by Cam Shepherd to win by the narrowest of margins, but thankfully this time a one-point win in our favour. It was a highlight playing against the legendary Tana Umaga in this game. He's someone who I had followed for so many years, it was a real thrill to play against him. At one point during the game, after a few scrum collapses, Tana (who was the captain at the time) ran in from the centres to tell the ref that our loosehead was clearly dropping his bind. The ref looked at him somewhat bewilderedly and Brendan Canno quickly told him to get back to the backline as he had no clue, to which Tana replied with a laugh, 'I'm just having a guess mate,' and jogged back into the centres. I had a good chuckle on the side of the scrum. You sometimes wonder if anyone knows what's going on in that front row at scrum time. With all the narrow losses we had at home, we were so thankful our supporters remained loyal. The crowds still averaged around 25,000, and it was great to finally give our dedicated fans a victory to cheer about. We finished the year seventh overall, and defeated a few big teams along the way, so it was definitely a strong progression from our previous year.

By this time, I had moved in with Pat O'Connor and Scott Daruda in the beach suburb of Scarborough. I was still learning more about what it meant to live with other guys and keep the house clean and tidy. We were pretty good about it, and would generally share the cooking— although I often made myself dinner as the other two weren't so keen on kangaroo meat and I was not a pasta fan. In hindsight, I was not the easiest person to live with. I was still pretty new to living out of home and sometimes after a big day of training was happy just to have cereal and head to bed rather than help cook, clean or hang out.

Scott and Pat were great to live with though and we had a lot of fun. One of the funnier things we did together was grocery shopping. Arriving at the supermarket we would put a big bunch of bananas on the baby seat at the back of the trolley—Scott said that it was a sign we were single, just in case there was a chance of a supermarket romance with a fellow shopper. After groceries we'd play 'scissors, paper, rock' to see who had to ask the bakery for free bread, claiming a story that the other two got to make up. Scott and I invariably rigged it, and poor old Pat had to try and explain that he had a pet pig just out of town that really liked bread, then it was pet mice. It got more and more ridiculous until the staff at the bakery would see him coming and chuckle in anticipation.

My family had managed to visit once or twice during the year for games and I had been to Brisbane to play a few times, so I had seen them more than I did in 2006. But I still missed them. I was missing out on seeing my brothers regularly and getting to know them better. I was not the nicest brother in my last few years of school—being so focused on my goals by putting a lot of time into rugby and training, I didn't have much time for them then and I regretted it now. My brothers, who I love so much, are amazing people, so we enjoyed whatever time we did spend together. Morgan, my best mate from school came over as well for the Australian Surf Life Saving championships (he is a gun in the beach flags) and he stayed over for a week after that. It was great to have someone staying with me in Perth and we got out to Rottnest Island and snorkelled, but just generally hung out and rehashed good times, quoting lines from the movie *Anchorman* and spending time at the beach in between my training sessions.

We also started planning what became one of my highlights in 2007— a trip to Zimbabwe. It was Morgie's first trip to Africa, and I was so excited about getting back there and seeing family. We managed to fit in visits to a few orphanages (and gave them soccer and netball balls) between our jam-packed adventure itinerary of bungee jumping, white water rafting, time on my grandfather's game farm and playing tourist around the country.

While there, we met with a man who was helping to set up a community development project in a rural town called Nkayi and its surrounds, about 170 kilometres from Bulawayo. We weren't able to go out there because of the political tension and the government's paranoia towards foreign journalists, but we were given the rundown about what they were doing—the problems they faced, how the program was to work and the consultation they'd had with local community chiefs and community members—and it all sounded great. It was small but they were clearly doing some amazing work, for all the right reasons.

Back in Perth, I shared a lot of what Morgan and I had done on that trip with Luke O'Keefe during our many conversations down at the Wild Fig, our favourite café on the coast. Not long after that Luke and I began helping people in a more meaningful way by starting EightyTwenty Vision. It was a small gesture, but one that we knew could make a difference. We planned to make a trip to Zimbabwe the following year, but first I had another season of Super Rugby to get through and if that went really well I could possibly even stake a claim for the Wallabies, but it was all there to do and it excited me.

The 2008 season with the Force started in late December with the unfortunate 'Quokka incident'. During a trip to Rottnest Island, just off Fremantle, players were accused of throwing quokkas (a small marsupial about the size of a cat). A media frenzy began in Perth after an eastcoast newspaper broke the story. From my point of view, I could see why people were upset—animal cruelty is unacceptable and some of the allegations were terrible. Before heading off to bed, I had seen a few boys pick up quokkas that had got into our accommodation, but hadn't seen any thrown. The actual story eventually came out during a players' meeting. We just sat there until Richard Brown owned up to picking up some quokkas. He's probably the most honest person I know (maybe a little too honest), speaking his mind and offending people, but also charming them with his honesty. It also came out that Scott Fava had thrown one later in the night when he was drunk.

Richard Brown, or 'Brownie' as he is known to most, grew up on a property near Julia Creek in central northern Queensland and is fairly at home around animals. He thought nothing about picking them up for a closer inspection. However, Brownie and Scott were made an example of and fined $11,000 and $5,000 respectively, and had to do fifty hours of community service.

The incident brought so much press scrutiny on the Force, almost all of it negative. It was my first experience of this kind of media and how it affected the public's perception of you—even if you weren't involved. We had people ringing in and comparing us with rapists and saying we should all go to gaol, which I thought was harsh, given that most of the players had nothing to do with it. There was a very thick folder with all the emails and transcripts of phone messages left in the players' lounge so we could read them and see the negative impact the event had on the community.

It was a tough start to the pre-season and after Christmas we got time to focus more on the rugby. But that was interrupted by a fight that broke out between Haig Sare and Matt Henjak after a night out with a few of the guys. It left Haig with a broken jaw and Matt eventually lost his contract over the incident. I was not around when it happened so can't comment on what occurred, but I was disappointed Matt had to leave. I got on well with him and he brought a lot of energy to the team. It did mean that Chris O'Young returned to the Force, after a season with Glasgow in Scotland, and it was great to have Chris back in Perth.

When we finally got to play some rugby it was another up and down year with fairly mixed results. Again, our form on the road was impressive—with a second undefeated trip to South Africa setting us up well early on. We had more matches that were decided by one-point margins, but thankfully we were on the winning side of the ledger each time with those. There was a definite sense that we were progressing well, though from time to time we would have lapses. Then you could see how much it upset the coaching staff, particularly Mitch, but he always tried to look for positives and urged us to find solutions rather than mope.

Mitch left it entirely up to us to find the solution during half-time in our final game of 2008 against the Brumbies. We were playing at home, with the Brumbies up 22–7. Mitch came into the change room and said, 'Sort it out,' and just left, taking the other coaches with him. Most of the players were furious, but we rallied from it and eventually won 29–22. If he had planned it then it was a stroke of genius. But I think Mitch had just been so frustrated about what he saw as a lack of effort.

Chris O'Young had moved back to Perth when Scott, Pat and I were coming to the end of our lease and looking for a rental place. Scott, Pat and I were struggling to find a house to rent (not so easy when you put three young guys under twenty-five on the application), so we decided it'd be easier if there were just two of us on it. I ended up sharing a place with Chris, while Pat and Scott found a place to share. Living with Chris was so good for me. He is one of the nicest people you will meet, is really intelligent and a great cook. He taught me a few of his dishes, and they're now my go-to when it comes to cooking. He was a lot neater than I am but was good at communicating, so I would try and pull my weight if he ever brought it up. It was a great living arrangement, and gave me a place I could call home in Perth.

In 2008, after the 2007 Rugby World Cup, Robbie Deans became the new Wallabies coach. I was excited and I wasn't even in the squad. You could sense that there was a lot of expectation from players and supporters with this change, which was exciting. I was so determined to one day play for the Wallabies and was doing everything I could to improve as a player, so was very excited when I got a call from Robbie to organise a catch-up during the week that the Wallabies were in Perth to play the Springboks in 2008. When I met him and the other Wallaby coaches for a coffee at their team hotel, he told me that I should focus on the Under-20s and really enjoy my last year of age-group rugby. I eventually ended up captaining the Australia Under-20 team in Wales that year. It was great to be back with guys my age and spend time with mates from school. I roomed for five weeks with James Hanson, who I played a lot of age-group rugby with—he now plays for Queensland Reds. The team was based in Newport, Wales, and there wasn't a great deal for us to do. 'Gangs' formed and we managed to make a lot of our own fun, including dressing up and running a sort of 'gang war' in the hotel with an elaborate strategy of room raids, pranks and the occasional BB gun.

We narrowly lost to England in our pool match—hugely disappointing—and it was a tough game, with Will Genia tearing his medial ligament and Ben McCalman breaking his leg. The way the tournament was set up only the top team from each pool progressed, so we ended up putting 40-odd points on Fiji and then France in the play-off for fifth. It was a pretty disappointing result overall, but there were some good performances. Quade Cooper played well and there were a number of other guys who have since progressed further in

Super Rugby and the international level. We sometimes talk about the go-karting we did as a team activity. We were put into four teams and it was timed: an hour of racing, and whichever team did the most laps won. Quade is a maniac in a go-cart. He broke the lap record within a few minutes. Our Welsh bus driver also managed to get the cart around the track faster than a lot of the lighter guys in the team. Sam Wykes was a sight to behold. He looked like a teenager riding a toddler's toy car, screeching and squealing around the corners.

After getting back from Wales, I had a few weeks of training with the Force before heading on a five-week development tour of the UK. I was loving it—travelling and playing rugby—and I felt like I was improving my game, so it didn't faze me to pack my bags and head back to the UK. It was a gruelling tour with a young squad, but one that we learnt a lot from. It was my first time captaining the Force and I enjoyed it for the most part, although it's hard to really enjoy it when you lose most of the games. We beat the Newcastle Falcons, but then lost to Saracens, Northampton and Leicester.

Before the tour I had made last-minute plans with Morgan to climb Mount Kilimanjaro the week after the tour. We had talked about it before, and then all of a sudden we decided to do it and booked ourselves on a guided climb. Morgs would meet me in Tanzania and I would fly down after the game. So the day after our last game against Leicester I was in Tanzania, catching a beaten-up old taxi late at night after my organised transfer was a no-show. It was the start of an adventure, so I didn't mind at all and ended up having a great time, playing the taxi driver's tapes as loud as they would go while he told me stories about the area and dodged potholes and cars without lights as we drove. It was a couple of hours of fun-filled driving adventure and we got lost several times, but he eventually got me to the resort just outside of Arusha. There I met up with Morgan and the rest of the climbing group to start the climb the next morning.

There were twelve of us in the group from all over the world. It was an amazing six days of climbing and getting to know them, playing UNO in the big eating tent at night with slight altitude-induced headaches, walking *pole pole* ('slowly slowly' in Swahili) towards and then up this enormous mountain, the highest in Africa. The group laughed when Morgs and I told them we had never really done any mountain climbing before. We had actually never even worn our hiking boots before. I had bought mine a day or two before leaving for the tour. Morgs didn't think 'walking in' his boots sounded like fun, so he didn't. We were there for the adventure, for the experience and we had such a good time.

Our water froze before we'd really even got into the serious climbing on the final night of the ascent because we didn't have the proper insulated Camelbaks. It was the coldest I've ever been with temperatures getting down to minus 17 degrees celcius and neither Morgs nor I having the correct gear for the climb, we just had our Brisbane and Perth winter gear and a big down jacket that we had hired in Tanzania, but we did have a lot of enthusiasm and were loving the adventure. Then for the last three hours to the summit we got separated from the tour guides, who had to stretcher someone off the mountain—he'd become delusional because of altitude sickness. But Morgs and I just kept going towards the summit. We were both really battling with the altitude and I think the dehydration added to this. Had we been with a guide we probably would never have been allowed to continue, but we were determined. We knew that only 30 per cent of people who climb Mount Kilimanjaro actually make it to the Uhuru summit, which is 5895 metres above sea level, and we were determined to be part of that 30 per cent. There was no way we were returning home having almost made it, so, stupidly or not, we struggled along the top of the crater to the official summit, walking ten steps or so and then sitting down to rest for a while before walking another ten or so steps, before resting again.

We eventually made it. To this day, it is the most exhausted I have ever been. We didn't look around for too long and, without even a smile, got someone to take a photo of us in front of the official summit sign before heading straight back the way we'd come. All we wanted to do was get off the mountain. Even going downhill was hard work, but at least we weren't going higher. Just over twelve hours after leaving the camp at 2AM, we staggered back into it, severely dehydrated and ready to collapse onto the thin foam mattresses in our tent. But it wasn't long after we'd stopped that I started spewing up what looked and tasted like my stomach acid, an almost fluoro green liquid that burned on its way through your throat and Morgs continued to cough a bit of blood, which he had started to do hours earlier, not far from the summit.

One of the guides took one look at us and told us just to keep walking: 'Just follow the track and keep going down the hill. Stop at the next camp.' We were only too happy to. You could feel the air getting thicker as we headed down and slowly started to feel a bit better. The guides brought our tent and backpacks down to us. The next day we covered the same distance it had taken us six days to travel on the way up, and were off the mountain to have a celebratory dinner with the rest of the group. Only half of the group had made it to the summit but it had been the experience of a lifetime. Morgs and I had conquered Mount Kilimanjaro and met some amazing people who we still keep in contact with every now and then.

After returning to Australia, I was back into training and I soon got a call to say I was in the Wallabies train-on squad for the Spring Tour. I had lost five kilograms on the climb and needed to put that back on as soon as possible. I went to Brisbane after a week or so and trained there—it was technically 'active rest' for the Force squad so we could train wherever we wanted.

I can't remember much about being called up by the Wallabies for the 2008 Spring Tour, but I know it was a phone call first of all.

My mother recalls it more readily and in a bit of detail: 'Dave was at home in Brisbane on a break, and his brother Steve was playing in an Under-16s Queensland Tournament at the time, so we were out and about watching those games. It was a Saturday afternoon and we were at home in the TV room. The phone rang and we hear, "Hi Robbie, yeah, thanks very much Robbie." We jumped up and, in silence, just watched [him take] the call. Once the call was over, Dave leaped off the couch into his dad's arms for a hug, with a beaming smile on his face.'

My family and I then went for a typical 'Pocock boy' walk in the park, with the staffie on a lead and a rugby ball being tossed and kicked as we walked together. There was lots of discussion and chat about the amazing opportunity and achievement—the sacrifices along the way and the blessings too. The squad announcement day on 23 September 2008 was the six-year anniversary of our arrival in Australia, so we went out for dinner as a family and then for a ride on the Brisbane Ferris wheel. One of the few moments of this time I clearly recall was during the Ferris wheel ride—I was subjected to a stinky fart from my youngest brother Steve at the top, much to his delight in the enclosed space. The things you remember from momentous occasions.

# 6.
# Defining Moments
## My Test debut and a new worldview

I t was quite surreal that George Smith, who I idolised and whose poster I had on my wall while growing up back in Zimbabwe, was now one of my Australian teammates. George was great when I joined the Wallaby squad. We had played against each other a few times during the Super 14, but I had never had too much to do with him. He was really friendly and when I was named on the bench for my Wallabies debut, he was one of the first guys to congratulate me. That approach never changed, even in 2009 when I started ahead of him in one or two games. He always said, if I needed help with anything or wanted to talk about stuff, he was there—and that meant a lot, as a young guy. Having someone like George, who is hugely competitive and obviously very good at what he does, still be prepared to help me, someone who other players might see as a threat and might try to shut out, I guess it says a lot about him as a person. All the guys loved George—he was a fairly quiet character who just liked being around the team and having fun.

My Wallabies debut in 2008 was against the All Blacks in Hong Kong—the first Bledisloe Cup game held outside of Australia and New Zealand. The build-up week was great and I was just so excited. My family weren't able to get there for it, but my then-manager (and still good friend) Richard Colreavy came over and so did Mitch, who was still the head coach at the Force. I was loving the Wallaby team environment and training with Lote Tuqiri, George Smith, Stirling Mortlock—guys I had watched play for the Wallabies for what seemed like a very long time. I ended up getting on for the last seven minutes of the match.

I still laugh every time I see photos from that week or from the game. I hadn't had a haircut for a couple of months and it was getting way too long, but where do you get your hair cut in Hong Kong? I made the mistake of allowing Drew Mitchell to cut my hair. He had opened up a 'salon' on tour called 'Jackson's' ('The original and best', he claimed). Quade Cooper and James O'Connor started up a rival hair-cutting operation called 'Joeys', a name derived from James carrying around 'Wally' the joey mascot. Drew stitched me up with a G.I. Joe kind of haircut. It was very short.

A few of the boys had bought BB guns and the first half of the week, outside of training hours, was crazy as 'gangs' roamed the team's floor of the hotel shooting at each other. They left fair-sized welts. Luckily sanity prevailed, and after a day or two the BB guns were put away before someone got hurt, but the friendly combat didn't end there.

One of the highlights of my week leading up to the game was the night Adam Ashley-Cooper made an elastic shooting device with a pen and a rubber band and we started shooting each other with rolled-up pieces of paper. They stung quite a bit. We improved the shooter contraption, and it got more and more intense, before eventually shirts were off and shots were taken from five metres away. Then Adam got me with three shots that drew blood. I was pretty surprised and suspected something. I found a small safety pin head that he had used instead of the paper. Our washing came back with safety pins and little tags on them, and Adam had collected these and broken their heads off. It was things like this, in the intensity of preparing for a Test match (especially being my first one), that helped ease the nerves and get my mind off the game for a little while.

The Wallabies then set off for the 2008 European leg of the tour. My mum and dad had decided to backpack and follow the team around Europe. They had been pretty busy since we moved to Australia and it was a welcome break for them. It was great to see them over there, like crazy uni students, getting around and seeing the sights and having a lot of fun.

I came off the bench late in the game against Italy in Padova, which is near Venice. The game ended up being fairly close before Quade Cooper pulled out his razzle-dazzle when he came on to score a Test try on debut and we ended up winning the game. James O'Connor and Sekope Kepu also made their debuts in that match.

A major tour highlight was beating England at Twickenham. Unfortunately I didn't play, but it was great to be in the stadium and experience the atmosphere. I was then on the bench for the match against France, but both Lote Tuqiri and I never made it on. It was the first time I had been in a twenty-two and not made it onto the field since I had started playing rugby, which was a weird feeling. You're obviously happy about the win but feel a bit empty because you hadn't played a part in the game. And inevitably, you get flogged in a fitness session on the field while your teammates enjoy the winning atmosphere in the change room.

We beat France at Stade de France, where the atmosphere was amazing. I had never heard such loud whistling, and *allez le bleu!* echoed around the stadium for a large part of the game. In the final game of the tour, I enjoyed some time off the bench against the Barbarians at Wembley Stadium in London. It was my first decent amount of game time in a Wallaby jersey and I loved every minute of it.

But, as the tour drew to a close, my thoughts quickly drifted away from rugby to where my new passion was developing—helping the Nkayi community in Zimbabwe.

Following my trip with Morgan the year before, Luke O'Keefe and I began planning and liaising with a few people in Bulawayo to go back in 2008 and find out more about what we could do to help. We ended up visiting a number of projects and hearing more from Anania, the project co-ordinator, about the work being done out in Nkayi. Anania had grown up in Nkayi and had moved to Bulawayo after school, working his way up from an auction yard to owning a successful cattle-rearing business and being the go-to man when it came to cattle in rural Matabeleland province. He is one of the most humble people you could ever meet and his good character shines through.

Things were still very edgy politically, so there was no way we would be able to get out to Nkayi. Instead we drove to Mosi-oa-tunya, which translates as 'the smoke that thunders', more commonly known as Victoria Falls. On the way, there were a ridiculous amount of roadblocks, with army personnel blocking access to side roads that led to rural villages.

There had been a lot of press, particularly in the UK, about the plight of rural Zimbabweans. The people were starving and the government seemed hell-bent on ensuring that it didn't get any more bad media attention. We saw countless kids on the road, picking up grain that had fallen from trucks carrying maize or eating berries from trees. Apparently that's all they survived on. Humans have the capacity to do some very terrible things and we were witnessing the effects of greed for money and power. Luke and I did a video blog and tried to find out as much as we could, but we left feeling deflated and sad. There had to be more we could do and we were determined to find a way to be of assistance and do something. We now knew about the plight of many people in rural Zimbabwe and felt like we had to try to help in some way, we could not just forget them and get back to our lives in Perth. Mother Teresa said that 'We cannot all do great things, but we can do small things with great love', and Luke and I hoped that we would be able to help in our own small way.

The following year in 2009, my personal and professional life changed a lot. From a rugby perspective I managed to play in every Force match and I commenced a timeshare arrangement of sorts with George Smith for the No. 7 jersey with the Wallabies. George was so humble about it the few times I was selected ahead of him. He retired at the end of that year after an amazing career. I felt very honoured to be the one selected to fill the massive void left by him—they were huge shoes to fill.

We had fairly mixed results during my first full year with the Wallabies, winning only seven of fourteen Tests played. But a major highlight for me was cementing the starting No. 7 position across five of the last seven Tests. The Spring Tour was a tough one when we went over to the UK and Ireland, hoping to secure the first grand slam tour since 1984. We got off to a good start, beating the English, but then drew against the Irish at Croke Park after Brian O'Driscoll scored on the buzzer to draw the game at 14–14. Although I won Man of the Match (my first with the Wallabies), it was bitterly disappointing to draw after a pretty solid game as a team.

I was rested for the next game against Scotland and was asked to do some 'special comments' at half-time and after the game for the BBC. I had never done this before, but our media manager, Matt McIlraith, thought it would be good for me. Keith Wood, the legendary Irish hooker, was also on the panel, so I was excited about that. I don't think anyone expected what came next—the Scottish beat us in a game that was pretty hard to watch, let alone make comments on. It was great to meet Keith and they made it fun, but for the Wallabies this was as low as it had been in my time with them. The guys were shattered and annoyed—and were given a good talking to by the president of the ARU, Ron Graham.

The only consolation was the fact that we had one more match left on our tour, against Wales, to try and turn things around. And this match holds some enjoyable (yet painful) memories for me. I was savouring the whole experience of playing at Millennium Stadium in Cardiff, which is an amazing ground, and the atmosphere was breathtaking. The Welsh sing like no other crowd I know and are so knowledgeable about and appreciate the intricacies of the game. A good scrum or rolling maul gets thunderous applause—you can't imagine too many Aussie props who have heard the scrums being applauded in Australia.

I found the Welsh crowd energising and had got stuck into the game and even crossed for my first Test try. But about ten minutes from half-time I came out from a ruck with my thumb bent to the side at ninety degrees. I hadn't realised it till I saw it and I wasn't sure what to do. I gestured for one of the physios or the doctors to come over, but then decided to just try and get it back into place. Play was still going on and I wanted to get back into things. I gave it a solid yank and it popped. It was back in normal thumb position but hurt like nothing else. Play stopped and the doc came on to have a feel and ask me what had happened.

I was determined to stay on there, so they strapped it up and I finished the first half, but at half-time it was already swelling up and my grip strength was pretty poor. With a guy like George Smith on the bench, you're not exactly going to keep playing at 90 per cent, so the medical staff made the call and my night was over. I had scored my first Test try, and was loving being out there, so I was pretty disappointed not to be able to finish the game. But I did get to sit back and enjoy watching a good second half display by the team, in which George featured prominently.

After the game, Warren, the Wallabies doctor, said that while I got the thumb back into place ok, please could I leave such things for him to do as he was the real doctor and there could be more damage if it's not done properly. I agreed, but in the heat of the game it was the last thing on my mind. All I knew was that my thumb was not how it should be and there was a game of rugby to play.

The next morning I had x-rays before we left, and they revealed I had broken my thumb in a few different places. But it was the end of the tour anyway. I was due to stay in Perth for only two days after returning from the tour, and then head to Zimbabwe with Luke for our agreed trip, so it was a mad rush getting in with a hand specialist. The specialist did some more scans before finally deciding that instead of putting a pin in it he would just put me in a plastic cast for six weeks. This meant I could still fly to Zimbabwe as scheduled. I went over there with my thumb in a cast and my ring finger in a splint from dislocating it a month or so before Spring Tour but not giving it a chance to heal. It was a painful start to the trip, but nothing compared with the pain of others that Luke and I would witness again in our Zimbabwean travels.

On a more personal note, 2009 was also the year I met my wife Emma. It was also when Luke and I finally brought our charity, EightyTwenty Vision, to life. Both have changed my worldview forever, and both inspire me to greater things.

Emma and I were set up by a friend, Jarrod McKenna, although Em didn't realise that until about a year after we met. I'd seen her at a vigil for the homeless, held at Parliament House in Perth, a few weeks before we were introduced, so it didn't take us long to get chatting. We became reading buddies not long after. Our first book together was *Mere Discipleship* by Lee C. Camp, a book exploring the political message of Jesus, discussing how political his life was when read in context, and what that meant for people today who wanted to follow his teachings. I hadn't met too many people my age who were exploring similar things so it was pretty exciting.

Jarrod, a mate in Perth who worked with Em, had whispered to me just before introducing us: 'Maybe wait a year before asking her out.' I wanted to give him a good punch on the shoulder but he was about to introduce me, so I glared at him and he just smiled. It was very sneaky of Jarrod as we had never discussed him introducing us before and I hadn't known I would meet Em then. I'm obviously really glad Jarrod did introduce us and he remains a great friend. He inspires both of us with the work he is doing around community support in Perth, talking to people around Australia about non-violence and the ways that we can care more for the earth and our fellow humans.

Em and I began hanging out whenever I was in Perth and just became really good friends. From there, things progressed. I found her feminist ideas fascinating and they challenged me and I enjoyed learning and reading (I began secretly reading feminist texts as I found her feminism challenging yet fascinating and was beginning to agree with many of the things she was saying, but probably wasn't ready to admit it). We've since joked about the irony of a rugby player dating a feminist and a feminist dating a rugby player. Em says she likes to contravene stereotypes, so it's not an issue.

In May 2010, we started talking about getting married. We spoke to our parents, as well as Luke and Bec O'Keefe, and Jarrod and his wife Teresa—to see if they thought it was a good idea. Everyone was pretty overjoyed at the prospect (especially my mum who said, 'I've just got one question: When?'). I surprised Em by asking her to marry me on her favourite beach, giving her a copy of Luce Irigaray's *The Way of Love* as we hadn't looked at rings yet. We got married in Perth with our family and friends around us in December 2010. My pop (Mum's dad) had managed to make it all the way from Zimbabwe and my granny (Dad's mum) came from Canada so it was a wonderful day. It was especially nice because our dear friend Jarrod, who had introduced us, conducted the ceremony and shared a homily.

Emma and I have a lot of common interests and really enjoy reading. We had to buy three bookcases when we got married just to fit all our books. I mostly read books about ideas, or different schools of thought, or people who fascinate me. This includes a lot on or by

Gandhi, Martin Luther King Jr, Richard Rohr, John Dear, Desmond Tutu, John Howard Yoder, Tom Wright and others.

Since meeting Em, I've been reading a lot more about feminist theory and really enjoying having my way of seeing the world broadened by new ideas. One of my favourite books is Paulo Coehlo's *The Alchemist*. Em recommended it to me back in 2009, when I was in Japan for a Bledisloe Cup game on the way to the Spring Tour. I ordered a second-hand copy online and it was waiting for me at the hotel in London when we arrived and I read late into the night, waking up again at 4AM (thanks to jet lag) and just continued reading. It's a great fictional introduction to Jungian psychology and has sparked my interest in Carl Jung and his theories.

It's been a lot of fun getting to know Em. One of the things I enjoy about her is that she really doesn't care that much about rugby. She cares about it because it's my job, but her friendship and relationship with me isn't at all dependent on what I do for work. Before we met, the only thing she knew about rugby was that at one point George Gregan had been captain of the Wallabies and something about Stirling Mortlock (because, according to Em, he has a great *Bold and the Beautiful* name).

There are no boys in Em's family, so she has become her dad's 'honorary son'. She has spent hours sitting on the couch watching sport (usually golf, cricket or AFL) with her father, John—during one Ashes series she watched the entire thing through a pair of red children's binoculars. After this she promised her dad she'd take them with her if she ever went to a 'proper sports game'. So in round one of the 2010 season, Em was sitting in the shed end of nib Stadium in Perth, with her sister Jess and Jess's boyfriend Alex, watching me play against the Brumbies with her red binoculars. Jess says she had to keep reminding Em to watch the game because she kept trying to find me with the binoculars.

The next time she came to a game, she brought along a friend of hers. They had decided it would be a good idea, since neither of them knew anything about the game, to take a book and write down the rules as they saw them in action. They decided that being tall and bald gave you a leg-up in the franchise's power structure after seeing John Mitchell, who was then the coach of the Force, and Nathan Sharpe, the captain. They also made some names up: for example, the lineout became 'the leap', the scrum 'tunnel ball' and a ruck 'stacks on'. They even ventured to write some suggestions about changing the rules to increase the viewing audience, such as incorporating dance moves into the lineout, which could then be scored by a panel of judges, and if the game happened to be a draw this could decide the real winner.

Later that night, Sam Wykes, who was not playing, came up to me and said 'Hey bro, was that your missus here tonight, with that blonde girl? And they were writing in a book or something?'

I nervously replied that it was, to which Sam responded, 'That's weird, hey bro'.

'Yep, it's pretty weird,' I replied, and we both just stood there, nodding.

# 7.

# Battling Demons
## Personal challenges and the EightyTwenty focus

When our family moved to Australia in 2002, I developed a stress-related eating disorder. I was irrationally strict about what I ate and had a very skewed idea of my body image and what I looked like. Looking back at photos, I was ridiculously lean but in my head I was still not lean enough. It became almost obsessive. I remember bursting into tears on a few occasions when the family went out to dinner or when travelling and there weren't any healthy or ultra low-fat options to eat. I would be so embarrassed about creating a scene, but was unsure how to deal with my obvious anxiety towards food. In my head, I rationalised my behaviour by telling myself that having as little body fat as possible would help me perform better on the rugby field. But this was only the case to some extent and I knew that there was an underlying issue that I needed to deal with and the rugby thing was a good excuse to use. In hindsight, my diet was not about being healthy, but was something I had a lot of control over and I went to such extremes to maintain that control. This was possibly a response to the fear I experienced living in Zimbabwe for those last few years on the farm when I felt so powerless, and when we arrived in Australia I used it as a way to give myself a sense of control and certainty. I've worked on this a lot with a psychologist, as well as talking about it with Luke O'Keefe and Em, and have improved out of sight. But that doesn't mean I don't still have moments when I feel like I am getting fat or haven't done enough exercise.

I'm getting better at approaching diet and exercise in a more healthy way but it is definitely a process and often hard to articulate or for people to understand, even though many people in society, particularly young people, struggle with similar, and far worse, body image problems. One of the things that helped me change my attitude towards these issues was Carl Jung's ideas about our inner community and 'shadow self'. Jung talks a lot about how our self is made up of lots of different parts—an inner community—and how we are almost always ashamed of or do not like some of these parts and many of them cause us pain. Rather than dismissing or ignoring those parts, or trying to get rid of them altogether, we need to make peace with them, to acknowledge them and embrace these parts of ourselves. Those parts of our selves that we don't like are what make us human and they do not necessarily have to determine how we act. Jung said that the less we embody them in our conscious life the blacker and denser they become in our unconscious—they do not go away if we just ignore them.

Em has helped me a lot in this area. When I start to get distressed she'll always get me to think about what the real issue is—what is it that I am actually becoming stressed about and is it just expressing itself as irrational thoughts to do with my body image. Anyone who knows Em will know how much she loves to bake and cook. My eating habits have been one of the big challenges for her since we got married. Because of my work and my approach to food, she's modified the way she cooks quite a bit, to the extent of substituting apple sauce for butter—even in béchamel sauce. Megan Cowan—Pek's wife—will joke with Em about her cooking: 'David Pocock approved meals' or 'Does that have the David Pocock tick?'

It's always more challenging working on my body issues when I'm injured. In the past, I have not dealt with injury that well. I would become obsessed with how much training and fitness I was missing out on and what I couldn't do because of the injury. And I would worry about putting on fat. My thoughts just weren't helpful at all.

But with great support from Em and a more philosophical point of view with the help of Jung's theories, I have become a lot better. I have also grown a lot as a person while dealing with injuries over the past few years. One outlet that has helped me with this has been gardening. Since moving in with Em, after we were married, I decided to do more in the garden and learn more about it in my free time.

We have a friend who runs a permaculture business, designing and building gardens in Perth. Em and I asked him to do a design for our place and I was fascinated by how much there was to it. Permaculture not only encompasses agriculture, horticulture, architecture and ecology, but also economic systems, land access strategies and legal systems for businesses and communities. It intrigued me a lot. I remember the amount of chemicals we used on our farm back in Zimbabwe—horrid things that are no longer used in Australia like methyl bromide and nitrates and fertilisers that we applied by the tonnes every year. It was certainly not environmentally friendly but is, unfortunately, still fairly standard practice in many developing countries around the world.

Our friend's permaculture plan and my interest in gardening have given me a good way to switch off and spend some valuable time with Em.

Luke and I were also juggling with the start-up and early development of EightyTwenty Vision, in which Luke really played a major part. Em has also been so helpful and supportive of me and really believes in EightyTwenty and what we are trying to do with it.

Luke and I set up EightyTwenty Vision to help the people of Nkayi increase their ability to sustain themselves and their communities. I was so touched by my first trip back to Zimbabwe with Morgan, and then two more trips with Luke confirmed this was the area of the world where we wanted to partner with people to help make a difference.

Our aim for EightyTwenty is to achieve a sustainable future by collaborating with people with the aim of building their capacities so that they can empower themselves, rather than just trying to provide solutions from the outside. I think we often, mistakenly, think that we simply need to go and help people who are in poverty or are oppressed because they are incapable of helping themselves, but this does not acknowledge a person's amazing skills and resilience. When we actually join with them in their struggle we begin to experience the *Ubuntu* that Desmond Tutu so often talks about, the care for each other as humans, recognising that their humanity is inextricably bound up in ours and when one human suffers we all do. I have found that while Luke and I initially went to try and help out in Nkayi, we both have learnt and received so much from the people there and their amazing resilience and sense of community.

Nkayi is situated in Matabeleland North Province, with a population of about 111,000, and people are heavily dependent on subsistence farming and cattle-rearing to make a living. Like much of rural Zimbabwe, Nkayi has experienced severe food shortages, resulting in malnutrition, poor health and it is also very vulnerable to HIV/AIDS.

Our four focus areas for EightyTwenty Vision are currently food security, education, women's and children's rights, and health. The food security element largely revolves around helping to identify and secure clean drinking water and teach conservation farming in community demonstration plots. Farmers are then able to compare the results to their own traditional ox-drawn plough methods in their fields and switch to using the conservation farming method if or when they want to.

In many countries around the world, women and children's rights have long been violated and we decided to raise awareness in Nkayi by setting up training workshops about women's rights to education, health, food and inheritance, and offer basic business and entrepreneurial skills too.

Child protection committees responsible for the monitoring of children's rights are also being set up and run by the community, recognising the need for an awareness of children's rights.

Deteriorating health is a major worry as well. There are multiple issues to deal with, but we hope to focus on providing essential medical equipment so people can get more appropriate care and support. Complications arising from pregnancy or childbirth due to poor or inadequate conditions is the fourth leading cause of death for women worldwide, after HIV/AIDS, malaria and tuberculosis. Most maternal deaths and injuries caused by biological processes are preventable and almost unheard of in developed nations. This is an area where we have seen relatively large improvements with small concerted efforts and the problems are often not as hard to solve as they may first seem.

The community also decided that establishing an annual netball and soccer tournament for the schools in the area would be very beneficial for the children, with some teachers even saying it would increase enrolment if kids had these tournaments to work towards. This has been implemented and I was out in Nkayi for the tournament last year and it was a sight to behold. I marveled at the skill and ferocity of both the soccer and netball, played mostly barefoot on dusty fields. The tournament also drew a big crowd of people from the community, who cheered on with songs and chants. It was very special to be there and experience the community spirit first-hand.

One thing Luke and I committed to when we set up EightyTwenty was to send 100 per cent of all donations collected to work on the ground in Nkayi and not use any part for administration in Australia. We were determined to find new ways to do this rather than to use the familiar model of taking a percentage of donations to pay for running the organisation. I know when I first started to donate to non-government organisations I was very wary about the amount that was eaten up by operational costs. While I realise this is a totally necessary part of business and not-for-profit organisations, we're pretty keen to explore new models and hopefully we'll come up with something that allows people to donate straight to the work in Zimbabwe.

I didn't want to annoy the Force franchise and Perth community with what I'm sure some saw as my bleeding heart cause while setting up EightyTwenty. I imagined people trying to avoid me: 'Here comes Dave, wanting to get some money for starving people—here we go again.' I didn't want and still don't want to become that person. I want to be able to invite people into a discussion about how we live, how we think, rather than have everyone write me off as that guy who helps people in Zimbabwe. That's just where I found an opportunity to be useful. I don't want everybody to only support what I've been doing, but rather to get involved with helping others where they feel they can. There are many people in Australia who are doing it very tough and we have many issues to deal with as a nation, so I am not trying to just ask people to help out with our work in Zimbabwe at the expense of people in Australia—I am sure we can do both if we choose to.

I am really encouraged by companies that try to help others. One that I've come to be involved in is Gideon Shoes in Sydney. It was started by the Noffs brothers, Rupert and Matt. They were angry about how factory workers were being exploited and set up the company to make sneakers in Australia in sweat-shop free conditions. Matt Noffs and his wife Naomi work for the Noffs Foundation, which provides services for young people and their families dealing with drug and alcohol problems. They also run Sydney Street University, a free educational and recreational centre for young people. Matt and his brother Rupert use the profits from Gideon Shoes to fund their work with the Noffs Foundation, which was started by their grandfather, Ted Noffs, in Sydney. It's something I get excited about—people reimagining the world and how they live in it.

I met Matt in 2010 when they released their first Australian-made shoes and he has since been throwing ideas around about similar business ideas for Luke and I with EightyTwenty. At the moment, we rely quite heavily on donations. Donations are great and people can be incredibly generous. But it's a pretty unsustainable business model to rely on to undertake the work in Nkayi. I was really inspired by the Noffs Foundation's work and how the brothers have created Gideon Shoes in order to sustain a cost-bearing existence. Luke and I know we need to work towards something similar, but my busy 2010 playing schedule with the Force and the Wallabies have put those ideas on ice for a short while.

Thankfully our 2010 pre-season at the Force didn't have quite the drama of 2009—there was no quokka incident or sacking—but it still carried its share of challenges.

Matt Giteau's departure was a real shame. Gits's contract included a significant third-party payment from Firepower International, which claimed to have invented an additive for fuel that would reduce vehicle emissions and save on fuel costs. On the surface, it sounded like a great initiative and more than a thousand shareholders thought so too. They sunk over $100 million dollars into the company on the false premise that it would be listed on the London Stock Exchange and bring massive returns. But it was later reported in the *Sydney Morning Herald* that the additive was false and the payment never materialised. Tim Johnson, Firepower International's chief executive, was later reported to have taken the investors money and was apparently living the high life around the world, while the shareholders were left to wear the consequences of his failure.

It was very disappointing to lose Giteau from the Force, but he was very good about it, and announced it to the team personally before it came out in the media. We really appreciated that because obviously a lot had gone on with his contract throughout 2009.

Gits went back to the Brumbies for 2010, and that left our squad a bit thin in the fly-half area. Mitch and the coaching staff went about filling the void and managed to lure former Springbok and prolific Super Rugby points-scorer Andre Pretorius as our new marquee player. I remember seeing so much of Andre among the scorers for the eight years he spent with the Lions (and, at various times, the Cats) as I was growing up, and was excited at the prospect of playing with him.

Andre brought great enthusiasm and experience to the squad in the 2010 pre-season, and said he was in the best shape he had been in for years. But it all came to an abrupt end at training one day when he suffered what seemed like a fairly standard hamstring strain. Scans later revealed his hamstring had been torn completely off the bone and that was the end of his season before it had even started. I felt really sorry for Andre, but Mitch, true to character, was determined for us not to mope around about it and move on with our plans for the season.

The fly-half situation became worse when our back-up option, Mark Bartholomeusz, also suffered a neck injury. The Force management had little choice but to have quick meetings with the ARU to determine if we could replace our marquee player. Thankfully logic prevailed and it was agreed we could. Mitch then went about finding another fly-half for us in early 2010. That person eventually turned out to be one of his past players, David Hill. Mitch had coached Hill at the Chiefs in New Zealand and had a huge amount of respect for him. Hill had been playing with the Toshiba club in Japan but a loan arrangement was worked out so that he could play for the Force in 2010. He turned out to be a great addition across the season and played a big part in our two biggest wins, against the Crusaders and the Stormers in Perth.

Going into 2010, I had enjoyed a good break in Zimbabwe and trained a lot smarter in the pre-season. I was really happy with my condition, but in round one I tore a ligament in my finger. It would see me spend another frustrating stint on the sidelines. My good mate Richard Brown suffered a shoulder injury in the same match. So, amid all the injuries that the team had already suffered around fly-halves, both Brownie and I were out of the back row too. Luckily we had some great depth in the squad to fill our positions, but it was really frustrating not being a part of it. I was determined to deal with injury a lot better this time, so Brownie and I turned the negative around and used our recovery time to do another mini pre-season of sorts together—pulling sleds at training and really pushing each other. You never like being out injured, but that time with Brownie really invigorated me for what would turn out to be my best year so far as a professional rugby player.

Brownie is one of the most honest people I have ever met—he tells it as it is. When I first joined the Force, being seventeen and fresh out of school, I hardly knew how to take him with his cheeky, teasing and dry sense of humour, but we have since become really good mates. I found it very funny when my younger brother Steve was in the Force academy at seventeen and was also struggling with Brownie's humour. He was telling me one day, 'You know Dave, with Brownie, when he jokes, he's joking but there's also some truth behind the joke, so it might be funny but he's making a point', which Brownie often is, as he's very insightful.

Brownie and I have become such good friends that he was a groomsman and master of ceremonies at our wedding. It was a brave gamble of Em's and mine, but it paid dividends because he was very humorous.

Touring with him is also great when we are rooming together. We don't turn on the TV, and instead prefer to play a lot of music, the kind you'd hear on Triple J, music created by real musicians—not that mainstream stuff that has perfect-looking people lip-syncing to auto-tuned recordings, which makes you want to pour bleach into your ears. We often do yoga and meditation at night before bed too. We may be rugby players, but we do have our softer sides.

Brownie is one of those guys who gets out and does things. Some people will talk about things for years and never do them, but not Brownie. He'll wonder how hard it is to kite surf, and the next weekend he's out there getting lessons, seeing if he enjoys it.

When we were in Paris with the Wallabies in 2008, we hired bicycles with a few other players and rode around the city taking in the sights. We eventually got to the end of the Champs Elysees and the infamous traffic shemozzle of the Arc de Triomphe as cars navigate their way around it in what seems to be organised chaos. Car rental companies have insurance exclusions for the area because it is just so crazy.

We got there and just had to do it—we had to try and get around the Arc de Triomphe on push bikes. We slowly eased out into the maze of traffic and hooting horns. You kind of go and stop, and then go and stop again, but then when we saw a gap we just went for it. It was really quite intimidating, and after getting halfway around the big traffic circle we decided to pull into the centre for a break and photo opportunity.

We jumped our bikes up onto the sidewalk of the Arc de Triomphe for a bit of a break, but some *gendarmes* came running towards us remonstrating in French, telling us to get back onto the road, so we reluctantly pushed out into the traffic again and managed to get back onto the Champs Elysees but going the opposite direction. We made it in the end. A full loop around the Arc de Triomphe on a bicycle. I was quietly proud of that.

Brownie and I hired bikes again on the 2010 Spring Tour in Paris, taking in the sights and visiting the Musee D'Orsay. Then we couldn't resist another exploring ride, with no idea where we were going. We eventually stopped to have something to eat, parking out the front of a little patisserie. The meal was quite good, but when we came out there was only one bicycle. Someone had stolen our hired bicycle. The actual hire was a few Euros, a lot cheaper than the train, but they keep your credit card details and if you don't return it there's a hefty withdrawal, which we had to pay. It was quite comical because we had been eating close to the window the whole time, and hadn't stopped for long, but this someone was a professional and had obviously stolen a bike or two before.

Another one of Brownie's memorable escapades was a 'rockumentary' he claimed to be making about Rocky Elsom on the 2009 Spring Tour. At any team appearance or travel day, Richard would shadow Rocky and take random photos of him. They were almost always taken with the flash on to ensure his actions were really conspicuous, much to the amusement initially, but later annoyance, of Rocky.

The victories over the Crusaders and Stormers were highlights of another season of mixed results with the Force in 2010, and Mitch and the coaching team came under fire in the media quite a bit throughout the season. Pressure was mounting on the coaches, with us not achieving our potential, and there had been a few events that put the spotlight on the coaches, including disagreements between Mitchell and Mulvihill.

It was a tough situation to have Mitch still with a year to run as coach, but effectively being told he was not wanted beyond 2010. Richard Graham came on as assistant coach, and Mitch bowed out a year early, with Richard taking over for 2011. It worked out better for everyone in the end, allowing the Force to start building for the future and Mitch to take up a contract with the Lions in South Africa. During his first year he managed to turn the Lions around in the 2011 Currie Cup. He is still a really good friend and came to our wedding in December 2010 on a trip back from Johannesburg.

I also still speak to John Mulvihill every now and then, after he went to coach in Japan. He used to do a lot of extra work with players around skills—catch, pass, high balls, etc—and he was particularly influential to my development during my early years at the Force. He is someone I have a lot of time for—a very honest and smart coach, who has a great relationship with his players.

Beyond the 2010 Super Rugby season I was fortunate enough to be selected for the Wallabies and ended up playing every Test that year. There were a couple of great highlights from the season—like the win over the Springboks in Bloemfontein and beating the All Blacks in Hong Kong. That win over New Zealand was a really important one for the entire team after having not beaten the All Blacks for a while. It was great to see Kurtley Beale and James O'Connor really impose themselves on the game and not take a backward step despite some really intense pressure. The winning kick from James was such a relief to us all. I remember running over and giving him a kiss on the forehead, I was just so happy that we had finally proven we could match it with the best.

The tour that followed to the United Kingdom and Europe promised plenty after such a great win in Hong Kong, but a committed Munster team gave us a real shock on a miserable night in Limerick, and England beat us at our own game at Twickenham. It was a strange game against the old enemy, as they threw the ball around like very few England teams had done before, and we were caught out by a lacklustre performance in the first half. From that point we were chasing the game and, even though Kurtley put in a great individual performance, we did not combine well as a team. We learnt a good lesson from it.

A much better result came in our final clash on that 2010 tour when we scored a record victory over France (59–16) in Paris. That match was so intense for the first half, and the score was locked at 13–all at half-time. During the break, Robbie didn't say anything too extraordinary, just that if we kept at it and held onto the ball and held our shape, holes would open up. He wanted us to build pressure and the opportunities would come. After a few tries early in the second half, everything started to stick. We were getting quick ball in attack, and in defence not giving them much. Drew Mitchell and Adam Ashley-Cooper were on fire and put on a real show. We scored forty-six points in the second half while France scored just a single penalty goal. It was one of the most dominant halves of rugby I have ever been involved in during my time with the Wallabies and such a pleasing way for us to finish off the year as we were heading into a Rugby World Cup year.

On a more personal note, I was honoured to receive four fairly big commendations for my year with the Wallabies in 2010. The John Eales Medal was the biggest highlight, as my peers—the guys you play with and want to impress—voted for it. You want them to trust you and feel like they can fully rely on you. The People's Choice Award was also very humbling, knowing that the public had voted for me as their best Wallabies player that year, and the Rugby Union Players Association Medal of Excellence had real significance because it's for more than just on-field work—players vote for who they think is doing great work on and off the field. The nomination for International Rugby Board Player of the Year was also a great honour, particularly to be nominated alongside some pretty amazing players. Being nominated has made me more determined to continue to improve and hopefully be nominated again and win it. I am still really enjoying my rugby and I still get a buzz playing with guys that I grew up watching on TV, guys like Nathan Sharpe and Matt Giteau.

In 2010 I also signed up for Twitter, which I still have my reservations about. I can see how it's great for allowing fans to get more access to players and see parts of their day-to-day lives that they would not usually see but it still sometimes seems like a bizarre concept. I have also enjoyed being able to keep up-to-date on news and find out what people are saying about different issues, so I am starting to get the hang of it. A few weeks after signing up to Twitter, I ran through to the bedroom saying, 'Em! Em! Bob Skinstad is following me on Twitter!' Emma was in hysterics at the sight of me holding my phone up to show her where it said 'bobskinstad follows pocockdavid', like an overexcited little kid anxious for someone to acknowledge how excited they were. We have laughed about it a few times since then, but it was easy to get excited when my childhood idol had suddenly acknowledged he was interested in what I was doing.

Bob Skinstad, apart from his continued involvement in the rugby world with commentary and TV appearances, has set up The Bobs for Good Foundation in South Africa which aims to give hope, pride and dignity to children through the gift of locally made, leather school shoes to those who don't own school shoes. Bob's example has reminded me how important it is to not take the opportunities I have for granted. It reminds me of the obligation of sports people to give back to society.

During a school visit once, I was asked by a Year 10 student who I get my inspiration from. I started talking about how I often find people working outside of rugby very inspirational, particularly people who, once they had decided what they believed in, pursued that regardless of the cost. I gave the examples of Mahatma Gandhi and Nelson Mandela—two men who had achieved so much, for so many people, at such a great price to themselves.

In our study at home, Em and I have a picture of Gandhi on a collage that we did together and underneath the drawing of him is one of my favourite quotes: 'One needs to be slow to form convictions, but once formed they must be defended against the heaviest odds.' It's not saying that your convictions can never change, but if we do not act on them and stand up for the things that we believe to be important, then we do a great disservice to ourselves and others.

As the rugby year played out in 2010 I kept thinking about EightyTwenty Vision, and how we could keep it all going in a more cost-efficient structure while committing 100 per cent of all donations to Nkayi. Luke O'Keefe had been doing such a great job with everything and I often felt guilty for not doing enough, so I was very determined to play a bigger part during the limited off-season that we have in rugby.

I was also increasingly frustrated as I became more aware of the manufacturing process and the sorts of conditions that people are working in while making clothes, shoes, accessories, sports apparel and other things that we wear and use. My manager was approached by three boot companies to get me to sign a boot deal, but I just didn't feel I could, knowing the conditions for the workers in the factories where these kinds of things are manufactured.

From those frustrations, I came up with an idea to start up our own rugby boot company, with shoes that were being manufactured ethically, with all the profits going directly to EightyTwenty Vision here in Australia and overseas. Luke's background is as a business manager, and he had just left his job, so it seemed like the perfect time to start something if we were going to.

Knowing what Matt Noffs had done with Gideon Shoes, I rang him up and asked what he thought about making an ethical boot. He loved the idea and suggested that he and his wife Naomi would come over to Perth to discuss it further. That prospect really excited me, and it became quite a focus away from rugby in the months that followed.

# 8.

# Untimely Injury
## My Rugby World Cup dream almost shattered

Every year around New Year's Eve I like to look back at the year that has been and revisit what has happened in the year. What did I really enjoy? How do I think I've developed as a person? Am I making decisions that direct me where I want to go? I also like to look ahead and think about the year to come and what I want to focus on personally. What do I want to improve? What can I change? Am I becoming who I always wanted to become—not as David Pocock the rugby player, but as Dave Pocock the person?

I do look at rugby and my goals for the year. It's a big part of my life, particularly in a Rugby World Cup year. I know how motivated I am to do well in rugby and if I focus on my life outside rugby and pursue new challenges that reflect who I am as I continue to learn and develop, those experiences will flow into my rugby.

I usually write down all my goals and refer to them as the year goes on, then look back at them the following year to see what I achieved. I often set small goals along the way to help me aim for a bigger goal. When setting out my 2011 plans, aspiring to be part of the Rugby World Cup with the Wallabies was high on the list. And I wanted to be sure other important aspects of my life didn't go on hold completely. I really wanted to step up my contribution to EightyTwenty Vision and help Luke O'Keefe a lot more. Setting up the charity has been a long process and, at times, frustrating with all the red tape and obstacles, but it provides me with a lot of drive and energy despite being time consuming.

Advocating non-violence is an idea I had been reading about a lot during that time, mainly books by or about Mahatma Gandhi, Martin Luther King Jnr and Jesus. You just need to look at the state of the world at the moment, to see violence is definitely not the answer. Although non-violence often gets fobbed off as idealistic pacifism, I don't see the current strategies working—military forces being sent to countries when the 'west' thinks they need to intervene, waging wars that many people don't want, without improving the lives of most of the people that developed nations are claiming they want to help. Imagine if people put the same resources into non-violence training and community-building as they did into building weapons that have no other purpose than to destroy lives? I dare say the world would be a remarkably different place.

In 2011, I committed to living my life by the principles of non-violence and ensuring I reflected those principles when thinking about the world, in the way I spoke and how I lived. I understand how paradoxical and hypocritical it must seem, a rugby player trying to be more non-violent, but I think you can be both—a rugby player who plays a hard game on the field and someone who commits to leading a non-violent life off it.

I also wanted to include a time of personal prayer, reflection or meditation into my everyday rhythm, whether in the morning when I woke up, or at night before bed. Mum and Dad brought my brothers and I up in a fairly conservative Christian home. When I arrived in Australia, people asked if I was 'religious'. Religious, I would think—not a chance! It was a term that I often connected with negative associations—of people who recited Bible verses but screwed over the poor in their business dealings. Sure, I believed that the life of Jesus was an amazing example of something different, a way of living that put love first, but it seemed ridiculous as a child (and still does today).

I have always tended to avoid talking openly about my faith unless asked about it; I dislike bible bashers as much as the next person. I've found I do not identify that much with mainstream Christianity or most of its past and current injustices towards people in Africa and other non-western parts of the world. However, my faith is such a huge part of who I am now that I would be doing an injustice to myself to not mention it here. I love what Gandhi said: 'I like your Christ, but I do not like your Christians. Your Christians are so unlike your Christ.' It is sometimes cringeworthy and often just plain disgusting to see what some people justify by their Christian faith and their claims to follow Jesus, a non-violent person who spent most of his time with the poor. If Christ was about 'good news for the poor', then surely in today's world first and foremost that means food, shelter and dignity. In partnering with people who are stuck in poverty to help them to build their lives, EightyTwenty Vision became one such way for me to act on many of the things I was thinking and talking about.

As far as rugby was concerned in 2011—wow, what a year! ... potentially. I'm not one to get too excited about things before they happen but, seriously, this was a special year—the year of a Rugby World Cup. It was also a new season for the Western Force with a new coach, Richard Graham. I have a lot of respect for him and he was great to work with at the Wallabies. So there was a full season of the new Super Rugby and then, provided I stayed fit and played well enough to warrant selection, I could be at a world cup, a Rugby World Cup!

In the 2011 pre-season, the established players were quick to welcome some new names into our ranks. Richard Brown organised a pig on a spit for one of the early weekends. I was so excited. I couldn't remember the last time I was at a barbecue with a pig on a spit. I don't usually eat pork or beef, mostly chicken and kangaroo, but this was a celebration of sorts and I was going to be there.

Brownie sent out a text message to everyone and put up a poster at training that said all you needed were 'drinks, budgie smugglers, a towel and $10' (to cover pig spit hire and meat). He picked up the pig from the butcher the day before, and kept it on ice in his bathtub overnight. No bath for anyone in his house that night I guess.

Emma dropped me off at Richard's place at 10AM. Kitted out in my polka-dot budgie smugglers, towel and plenty of sunscreen, I was ready to enjoy the afternoon. Brownie had been up since 5AM setting up the pig and organising everything. It was a great day spent hanging out together and the meat was really delicious. The whole team didn't turn up, which was a bit disappointing. It wasn't compulsory or anything, though we usually tend to get a good turnout. When you are in a team environment, it's amazing how the group dynamic changes when certain characters are or aren't present, and it just seemed different with only fifteen or so of us there.

Still, we all had a great time and the next day we kept the summer theme going, spending most of the afternoon down at the beach with Emma and Richard and a few other friends. I wheeled my paddle board down and Brownie had his fishing kayak, so we all took turns on them. It was a really good day off after a hard week of pre-season training. Perth is such an amazing city with the beach so close by. The ocean has always captivated me. Growing up in a country surrounded by land, our family would only go to the sea for holidays once a year at the most. The waves, sand, rock pools and seagulls all just seem so magical.

Mike and Steve came over to visit in early 2011 and I had such a good time with them. You don't realise how special family are until you move away from them. I loved having both my brothers staying with Em and I and was able to spend quality time with them.

By the time the new Super Rugby season had come around, our squad was in pretty good shape and we had high hopes going into our first clash of the season against Queensland Reds in Brisbane. It's never easy playing as the away team at Suncorp Stadium and the heat on that day made it a pretty tough start to the season for both sides. We dominated for most of the match and James O'Connor had a great game, scoring all our points. But a yellow card in the 66th minute meant we were a man down for most of the final period, and the Reds came back hard and stole it from us 21–20. Yet another one-point loss, but it didn't matter how close it was because we really should have held on for the win.

It was a frustrating start to the season. We had a bye in round two so we couldn't make amends for at least another two weeks. Then we lined up against the Sharks in Perth during round three. It was this match that threatened to derail my Rugby World Cup dream. I remember it all vividly.

I was on the ball, the Sharks were in our 22 and I had found just the right timing and was trying to get the ball free from the tackled player. Jannie du Plessis tried to clean me out but glanced to the side, then grabbed my neck and pulled me backwards towards him. At the same time, I tried to fall back on our side to place the ball back. All I managed to do was flick the ball out to one of our players and he wasn't expecting it, so it went to the deck and Odwa Ndungane toed it through and scored early for the Sharks.

My foot was firmly in the ground and I couldn't move it because it was under another Sharks player—then I got pulled over it. It happens often and I wasn't too concerned about how I had been cleaned out. I just knew I'd heard a pop and my knee hurt a lot. I thought the referee should've blown his whistle to give us a penalty for their player holding onto the ball on the ground. Jannie got up and stood over me. I told him to get lost. Then he said, 'Next time, I'll break your fucking neck,' before one of his teammates, and a friend of mine, Tendai 'The Beast' Mtawarira, pulled him back towards the halfway line.

I remember the voice of one of the physios as he twisted and pulled at my knee, testing its integrity. 'Mate, it feels like you've done something, I'm afraid it feels like you've done your ACL.'

I stared up into the night sky. The crowd's cheers seemed to be more of a fuzz. This really couldn't be happening. I was helped to a seat and watched the rest of the game from the reserves bench.

I was furious. Fair enough, I had injured my knee—this happens frequently in a game of rugby union—but what was that verbal all about? You can't say things like that. I was so annoyed. I thought it was a malicious intent to injure—not to play the game hard and give out better than you get, but to injure. It went against everything I had grown up believing sport was about. Within the laws of the game you may do everything that you can to bash the opposition player, but you never wish an injury on him. In fairness, Jannie did come over briefly after the game to see how I was, but I was still filthy about it. The physio had told me that my season was over, so the apology seemed like no consolation at all.

The next day I tweeted what he'd said. I just thought it was such poor form and was still really annoyed. I was surprised how quickly it got picked up and it ran in a few stories in the next day or two. I got a call soon after from Mitch Hardy (our team manager). He said South Africa, New Zealand and Australian Rugby (SANZAR) wanted me to delete the tweet, which I thought was pretty silly. All I had done was quote someone. If they were so concerned about it, why not address what was said? You can't go making such threats off the field, so why is it ok on the field? It didn't seem worth making an issue out of, so I just deleted it, which is some sort of Twitter heresy I'm told.

Jannie called me the next day. He was genuinely apologetic. I accepted his apology and then we talked for a while. He is actually a really good bloke. We talked about how much we enjoy getting out of the city and how we often go out to the country to recharge. He and his brother Bismarck had grown up on a farm too.

We went on to lose against the Sharks. It was a horrible night. We were in it for a large part of the game but it blew out a bit and the Sharks deservedly recorded a good win. A losing dressing room is bad enough, let alone nursing what I still thought would be a season-ending injury. I tried my best to see most of the players. Often when you lose games it is not for lack of trying. It sometimes comes down to a few individual errors, which guys don't make on purpose, so it's important to tell your teammates that they put in a good effort. Not a 'well done, we came close enough', but more a 'keep your chin up, we will be better next week and not have to feel this.'

After doing that, I just hung out in the medical room. An MRI scan was going to be organised the following day and our head physio Rob Naish said that the hospital would call me in the morning. I was excused from the post-match function and could head straight home. I walked outside our change room to catch up with 'The Beast' and then went back inside to find our team doctor, Mike Cadogen.

'Doc, so what's the best case?', I asked.

'Best case is that you have just strained your medial and you'll be back in a few weeks,' he replied. 'Worst case is that you've done it all, [you'll need an] operation and you're looking at about nine months out.'

I didn't get to sleep at all that night. Finally at about 6AM I dozed off and woke just before 9AM, in time for a quick breakfast before leaving for the scan.

The MRI showed a tear in the medial collateral ligament and a small meniscus tear—a great result as far as our physios were concerned. I was still hugely bummed about missing six to eight weeks, but did think it was a lot better than missing nine months.

One of the really talented younger guys coming through at the Force, Justin Turner, did his ACL (anterior cruciate ligament) in 2010 and I'd watched him during his recovery: months and months of rehabilitation, copious amounts of upper body weights, upper body fitness on the grinder and boxing with Brendan Appleby (the Force's assistant strength and conditioning coach). It seemed like a very hard and frustrating slog. My heart went out to Justin when he did the same knee again in his first contact session back. All of a sudden, six to eight weeks on the sideline didn't seem so bad.

A lot of people asked me, 'What do you actually do when you're injured? You can't train can you?' Yes we can and yes we do! The week after my knee injury against the Sharks was one of the more exhausting weeks of training that I can remember. I was still in and around training and did five upper-body gym sessions and, while the guys trained and prepared for the Blues game, I was kept busy on the sideline, doing over 450 chin-ups in three days, with various push-ups and core exercises in between. There were a few injured players on the sideline so we worked together. I was physically and emotionally shattered.

Most athletes will tell you that the hard work is in the pre-season and preparation. The fun part, the reason why you do all the hard work, is to play. To get out on the field with your mates and go head to head with the other team to see who is better—to see if all the hard work pays off and you perform under pressure. Who will win? Do you have what it takes? Will you find that little bit extra when it gets really tough and pull through with the goods? After a game your teammates pat you on the back and tell you you've played well. There would be none of that for quite some time.

Throughout the rehabilitation period, I needed to find something to keep me occupied. It wasn't long before I was back in our garden. The garden has slowly come along, but working in it isn't always as soothing as it should be. The tradespeople who built our house had dumped builders' sand in the terraced garden beds rather than taking it away and putting in decent soil. Emma and I spent hours shovelling it out. What a bunch of corner-cutting good for nothings! I've cursed them under my breath many times as I pulled out yet another rusty metal pipe or piece of brickwork. All the while remembering my dad ranting about not doing half-jobs back on the farm. He didn't tolerate it at all and it seems I inherited that lack of tolerance for anything being half done.

While I was recovering from my injury, Emma and I spent a few days in Albany, Western Australia, with her grandparents. It gave me yet another taste of how beautiful it is in the south west. I've really loved the few times I've had to explore different parts of Western Australia. It's such a beautiful state.

But it didn't take long for reality to hit once we returned home. I had a follow-up appointment with the orthopaedic surgeon, Dan Fick. He just wanted to see how I was tracking and have a look at another scan. He was particularly interested in a section of my anterior lateral meniscus, because the first scan had showed something going on there.

I trained really hard that morning and pulled the sled for the first time since my injury, feeling more confident and stable on my knee, even though it was still in a brace. I hate pulling the sled, but loved it because I had done hardly anything on my legs up until that stage, apart from rehab and quite a lot of left leg press. I had to have another MRI scan, so I went straight from training to have that done before going directly to Dr Fick's practice. I just expected the standard follow-up and chat—he'd tell me that I could adjust my knee brace, maybe even get out of it, move on to more rehab and be running in a week or two. But things took a different turn and I was faced with a really tough decision that I wasn't expecting.

Fick studied the scans thoroughly, and pointed out a few things he was concerned about. He reminded me about the last time there was some damage. He wasn't sure if this was a new injury or pre-existing. Eventually he said he thought he should operate. I didn't know what to say. This was not how I thought the meeting would go.

'I could do it tomorrow afternoon, and if the damage is what I think it is, going by the scans, then it shouldn't affect your overall recovery time,' Dr Fick said as I sat there bewildered.

'There is obviously the risk that it is worse than it looks, but I'll only know when I get in there, and it's a call I'll have to make.'

We talked about the options with the Force's assistant physio, Merv Travers, for about fifteen minutes until I was sure that this was the right path and I fully understood the injury and what the plan was. There was a chance that if he had to stitch the meniscus to repair it, it would be three months out, but the potential consequences of just leaving it were a lot worse.

It needed to be dealt with as soon as possible so I could have time to heal and get back on the field. Dr Fick talked about the two scenarios that could occur when he operated. The first was that once he opened up my knee, it would be as he thought and he'd just have to shave the meniscus down and get rid of the bit that was torn. This was pretty standard and it would not take too long to recover. The other scenario, the one that I did not like the sound of, was that the tear was bigger than the scan showed and he would have to stitch the meniscus. It could then take three months to recover, with no way to speed it up. Dr Fick explained what he'd based his decision on, depending on what he found during the operation, and I felt comfortable about him making the call. He knew the position I was in and the pressure I had on me, externally as well as all the stress I put on myself, to get back onto the field for the Force. Then there was also the added incentive of it being a Rugby World Cup year. I was nervous, but figured time would tell and I'd make the most of either outcome.

I didn't sleep much after the meeting with Dr Fick. I am not usually the worrying type, but I felt uneasy. It would probably be ok and I'd be back playing in a month or so, but there was the possibility that the tear needed stitching. It's amazing how injury seems like a big deal in your own little world at the time it's happening, but if you get a broader perspective it's really quite insignificant, especially in light of what was happening in the world through the early months of 2011. The natural disasters occurring around Australia and the world—flooding in Queensland and northern New South Wales, fires here in Western Australia, earthquakes in Christchurch and Japan, flooding in Sri Lanka—and I am worried about my knee. You do feel silly sometimes, as a professional athlete, and I guess you need to get a bit of the big picture and have people in your life who help give you this.

I trained the next morning and rushed home to eat, as I had to fast from 11:30AM for a 6:30PM operation. I eat five or six meals a day, and I knew I'd be pretty hungry by that time so I had to get some food in beforehand.

Em picked me up after the surgery. I vaguely remember seeing Dr Fick after the operation, but I have no recollection of what he said. He had called Em and explained what he'd done and how it went. Em said that it went well. Dr Fick, who must've been tipped off about Em's feminist ethic, told her that it definitely should not excuse me from any housework and, indeed, that housework should probably be part of my recovery regime.

The next day I was feeling pretty out of it from anaesthetic and painkillers, and my knee was fairly sore. The Force gave me the day off, so I used it to do some work for EightyTwenty Vision. We were really busy re-doing our website. Since it is our only real marketing tool, keeping it up-to-date is pretty important. It's only Luke and I running things in Australia. We are so determined to keep the administrative costs down so that all donated funds go to the work on the ground in Zimbabwe, but this means we've been pretty busy. Luke has a full-time job so he fits in the majority of the admin work at night or on weekends, and I fit it in between training and on days off.

We had a lot to complete before the Force's charity match against the

Waratahs, which was raising funds for EightyTwenty Vision. The match was only two weeks away at that stage, so we spent time working out the details of the night and deciding how to maximise the opportunity. I was really disappointed not to be playing in the game. The work we are doing in Zimbabwe really means a lot to me, and the opportunity to play a game for the Force in a jersey that was specifically for EightyTwenty would have been very satisfying. But it didn't take me too long to realise it was not going to happen, and I needed to find ways to help raise money and exposure for EightyTwenty from the sidelines. Inevitably that meant a lot of talks and corporate suite visits before the game.

The charity match became a major focus for me for most of March 2011. I was also looking for ways to try and enhance my rehabilitation after injury. At a fundraising function in 2010 I sat next to Dr Alistair Nuttal, who uses hyperbaric chambers to help recovey from injuries. He heard that I was injured and contacted me about using it, so Emma drove me out to his clinic in Midland and Alistair explained the science behind it. There have been a few studies on sportspeople and some of them seemed to get results. Alistair is such an interesting man. He showed me how it all worked and it sounded like a good idea, so I was squeezed into a chamber for my first treatment. It would become a regular part of my rehabilitation in the weeks that followed.

Throughout it all, I kept training as much as I could, but my knee was still really sore and it was swollen for a lot longer than it was supposed to be. I wasn't expecting this much post-operative pain. Emma said she spoke to a good friend of ours, Penny Scott, who was the scrub nurse for my operation. Apparently they really had to dig around because my knee was so tight and that's what caused the extra pain. Penny said Dan Fick did the most meticulous job she's seen him do, so that was a relief to hear.

During my rehab most mornings began with a hyperbaric treatment down in Fremantle and some days I was in the big decompression room rather than an individual capsule. That meant I could take a book in. At the time, I was reading John Smit's autobiography, *Captain in the Cauldron*. I hadn't read a book about rugby for a long time. In the past, I'd read Jonah Lomu's autobiography and books on Tim Horan, Jonny Wilkinson, Carlos Spencer and Stephen Larkham.

In the week leading up to the EightyTwenty match against the Waratahs, there was a particularly poignant moment when I was doing my knee rehab in the gym. Nathan Charles was doing a fitness test on one of the rowers ('ergos'). It reminded me of why I enjoy playing rugby so much. Not him doing a row (I hate those rowing machines) but the kind of people you meet and become friends with. Nathan has a remarkable story. He has cystic fibrosis (CF), a hereditary disease that causes thick, sticky mucus to build up in the lungs, digestive tract, and other areas of the body. It is one of the most common chronic lung diseases in children and young adults and is a life-threatening disorder. Initially, he kept his condition a secret from every one except team doctors, not wanting it to hinder his chances of selection or having the stigma attached to people with 'diseases' that people know little about. However, Nathan recently took up an ambassador role with CF Australia and is now raising awareness about the disease. I have been fortunate to meet inspirational people like Nathan—guys who, to the public, are just faces on TV and are judged on how well they carry the ball or tackle an opposing player rather than how they tackle life itself. It was a timely reality check for me while I trained and thought how disappointing it was that I couldn't play in the charity match. People in our immediate playing squad were dealing with far greater challenges than mine.

# 9.

# Rising Again
## Returning from injury and charity challenges

April 2011 was another testing month on many fronts. I continued my injury rehabilitation and worked hard to ensure that the EightyTwenty Vision charity match against the Waratahs on 9 April was a success.

On the home front, our great friends, Bec and Luke O'Keefe, became our new neighbours on the first weekend in April and Emma wanted me to cook a barbecue to celebrate their arrival. I thought it was a great idea at the time, but I soon became stressed because I hadn't been able to do enough training. I can get like this sometimes—I get agitated when I feel that I am not working hard enough or am not doing enough to stop falling behind, physically or skills-wise. I have to do everything I can to keep on track.

When I was in Year 11 at school, I was injured and missed the entire rugby season. My poor family had to put up with a lot from me. I was often in a foul mood and was not very pleasant to be around. I have since realised just how destructive this behaviour is to my emotional health and for the people around me—so I try a lot harder now to control my agitation and instead try to use it to motivate me.

Since we've been married, one of the big learning curves for Emma and I is getting the balance right between training and home time. For me, I am trying to make enough time for Em and the other things in my life outside of rugby and for Em it is trying to understand my training/ work schedule and what that entails. We tend to strike a pretty good balance now, but it's always something we have to work at.

I guess that's something that the public may not really understand about what happens when a professional sportsperson is injured. There's this idea that when we're injured it's a bit of a holiday, but in lots of ways you end up doing more work than in the normal training cycle. You have to do your injury rehabilitation, your regular (or modified to manage your injury) weights, some kind of cardio, watch the field training, your normal and injury-related physio and massage. I find that on top of all this, I feel a bit guilty watching my teammates busting their gut on the field on the weekend and not being able to do anything to help them.

I felt that guilt after our at-home match in April against the Melbourne Rebels. It was yet another agonising one-point loss following so many opportunities, but we just made silly mistakes. The boys were gutted, as were the fans.

I hate losing. To take my mind off it, I woke up the next morning and went to the gym with Em. I managed to do forty minutes on the cross-trainer in my leg brace, which was what the physios said I could do, so I was pretty chuffed about that. After that I did some weights and then headed home to ice my knee before heading back down for another session in the hyperbaric chamber in the afternoon.

In the evening, we had the O'Keefes over for their welcome dinner. Their boys, Zach, Sam and Kalen, were so excited about the move. When they came over and realised Emma was cooking them pizza for dinner, they danced around the living room for half an hour and kept wanting me to put 'dance music' on. They would stop dancing and complain if the music wasn't upbeat enough.

Zach is the eldest. He is incredibly intelligent and loves telling stories. Zach's also incredibly melodramatic and everything he feels he expresses with his whole body. It's quite comical to watch and sometimes Emma and I get the giggles when he is trying to communicate his frustration or dismay, which probably isn't the most appropriate response from 'grown-ups'.

Zach is especially lovely when he's helping his brothers. Whether he's helping Sam get to the next level on *Super Mario Brothers* or helping Kalen get down off a chair, he's always committed to helping people who can't quite do what he can, which is a delight to watch.

Sam is six and is incredibly funny, cheeky and athletic. He loves playing, especially with his brothers. He also loves saying the words 'poo', 'bottom' and 'wee' whenever possible. He even renamed Emma Mrs Bottomface at one point. We were the Bottomface family. While Zach's best friends are girls, Sam has an apparent disdain for them. He declared that Emma couldn't help them move in next door 'because she's weak', for which he received a merciless tickling from the two of us.

This part of Sam is so much fun because he is already learning how people work and what makes them comfortable and uncomfortable, and he's confident enough to test those boundaries. Sam is at his best though when he is working hard at something he's good at. He gets this look of determination and you know that he is going to master whatever skill he is attempting, whether it's drawing, reading or colouring in the lines.

When Luke and Bec had their youngest boy, who is now two, they decided to name him Kalen David O'Keefe using my name as his middle name. I was really honoured.

But they've been lamenting that decision because in an uncanny way it seems to have produced some pretty unusual behaviour in Kalen. He is frequently complaining of sore feet or sore toes, much like myself (I've twice had my big toenails removed after perpetual problems with them being stomped on during games and training).

Kalen is very determined and quite a tough little character too. He can be running full pelt and 'clothesline' himself on something he obviously feels should move for him. Then he just dusts himself off, looks around, laughs and carries on with his original course of action. When I dismantled the spa deck to remove the spa and create more space, he had his own little screwdriver and 'helped' me for about two hours. He took off all his clothes in that time and just cruised around the garden starkers. I often come home to find him chatting away to Emma, proclaiming 'car' or 'plane' every time he hears one, or talking to her about 'the woggles' (the Wiggles) or asking ''sthat?' (what's that?)—it's his favourite question.

It was great having the O'Keefe family move next door. But that Sunday welcome dinner became a painful experience as the night wore on. I started to feel really sick during dinner, and by the time our guests had gone home I was feeling particularly bad. By 11PM my stomach was aching to the point where I was just curled up in the foetal position. Em took me down to Sir Charles Gairdner Hospital where the Force team doctor, Mike Cadogen, works as an emergency doctor. I was having a reaction to some of the pain medication I'd been on after the operation and so he put me on a drip and got me some other medication as well. We ended up getting home at about 12.30AM and I had a really interrupted sleep with a lot of pain throughout the night.

Em insisted on driving me into training the following morning, which was lucky as I fell asleep on the way. I managed to do some weights and light training before seeing the doctor again. Then Em picked me up and made me go to bed. I often think sleeping during the day is a waste of time but Em was adamant that I needed to rest. Sure enough I was fast asleep after not very long. It was a good thing that she did—otherwise the week ahead would have caught up with me at some point, given we were so busy organising the EightyTwenty Vision charity match.

The Western Force were fantastic in supporting the match. Luke and I are learning as we go, so it must be frustrating for the Force. We are a pretty tight organisation and Luke carries most of the load.

Things are getting really busy so we're looking at ways we can rethink the whole 'We're a charity, please give us your money' model.

We don't want to limit what the charity can do because of the amount of donations we receive, which, in the early months of 2011, had been very little. And we definitely don't want to take a share of what people gave us to pay someone to do administrative work. We brainstormed various ways around this and from there we started to progress with our plans to investigate making an ethical boot with the Noffs brothers. By this stage I had become an ambassador for Gideon Shoes. I spoke to Matt early in the year to explain the boot idea, which he really liked, and said he'd come over to Perth with his family to discuss it further. So we locked in the date of our team bye in May as the weekend to work on the boot concept together.

Having those plans in place put me at ease a little about the future funding EightyTwenty Vision. I was getting excited about offering alternatives in the sporting apparel market, making boots that respected everyone in the production process, and didn't just make a company a lot of money but left workers earning a pittance. This would have to wait though, because the immediate focus was on the charity match against the Waratahs, which was now only days away.

While I continued to work with Luke on logistical requirements around the charity match, my injury rehabilitation became a lot more responsive after sorting out the pain medication. Training became more satisfying. I did a running session, and it's amazing how much better I started to feel after a bit of running. You start to feel like you're improving, and you do the rehab running next to the training field, watching the boys train. It's a step closer to being back with the squad.

The day before the match against the Waratahs, I found myself at a charity event as a sort of guest speaker, discussing my experiences with a charity. Richard Brown had been asked to help get tables together for a Youngcare cocktail party. Youngcare lobbies, fundraises and provides funding for young people with disabilities who have to live in aged care facilities because there are very few facilities specifically for them. I was asked to talk a bit about the challenges we've faced in setting up a charity and how things were going, which I was happy to do. But I felt a bit strange talking about EightyTwenty Vision at another charity's fundraiser. I tried to focus on the mindset of not making charity just a one-off donation or dinner, paying off our consciences and then getting on with our everyday lives. I talked about re-thinking the way we live and how we can be more community minded and inclusive, as well as more giving. The talk seemed to go down fairly well and it was probably quite good timing to be sharing that period with others rather than worrying about the challenges we faced the next day. It helped for a better night of sleep.

The next morning I started with an interview on a local radio station. All preparations that could be done up to that point were done, so after the interview I looked for something different to occupy my mind for a couple of hours.

A really good fruit tree nursery was having the last day of a 20 per cent off sale, so I borrowed Brownie's ute, 'Smokey', and a cage trailer and off we went to buy fruit trees. I love driving Brownie's ute. It's an old Ford that runs on LPG. You can't just cruise along, you have to really drive the thing, making sure you rev high enough to keep it going at traffic lights and maybe even throwing in the odd double de-clutch for good measure. None of the locks really work, winding up the windows is quite the workout and it looks like a car that has been through a lot in its time—it has character! Brownie bought it for a grand or two so he could get onto the beach and take his kayak with him. I feel cool driving it. Emma thinks it's hilarious and that it's probably a reflection of my past—growing up in Zimbabwe, driving around the farm in the old, barely-roadworthy LandCruiser, or my dad letting me drive home from school with him when I was just twelve, on main roads and all.

Our fruit trees made it home and Brownie's ute held up ok. By late afternoon there was no further time for distractions. We had to be ready at the stadium around 6PM to see all the volunteers who were collecting money and get the run sheet for all the things I had to do, mostly Q & A's and meeting people, but it was tightly scheduled, with five of them in the space of little more than an hour. The jerseys at two of the auctions went really well, though one of them, which was a silent auction, went really cheaply. Unfortunately that wasn't the only disappointment of the night.

The Force have a 'Chairman's Lounge' where approximately ninety guests sit down before the game to a three-course meal with a few guest speakers—it's pretty fancy as far as a night at the rugby goes. Tables are generally bought by companies or given to sponsors of the Force (as part of sponsorship agreements), who then bring their clients or employees. This means the majority of the people there wouldn't have paid for their tickets. With this in mind, we decided we should put pledge cards on each table so people could give money. If you're at a free dinner and someone is raising money for a good cause, you feel obliged to buy a few raffle tickets or chuck twenty bucks in the hat as it's passed around. I went around collecting the pledge cards and personally thanked those who made donations, but out of all the people in there we received just seven donations. It was a far cry from the average punters with their families, who dug deep into their pockets and were very generous when putting money into the donation tins at the gates on the way in. I guess the wealthier people didn't get wealthy by giving their money away.

On my way around the tables an older gentleman shook my hand and said, 'Good on you for what you're doing, but I've always thought that we should put a roof over every person in Australia's head before we help anyone outside of this nation.'

I accept that many people share the view that we should look after those in our own backyard before we go and help anyone else, and I respect that view. Although I think we can and should do both, it really made me angry. I wanted to say, 'Yep, and that's why you invest all your money in building your own wealth? Because that is exactly what will help the one hundred thousand people who have to try to find any accommodation they can every night around Australia, or else sleep rough in squats or on the street.' I didn't say anything though, just thanked him for his support—everyone is entitled to their own opinion.

Adding to my disappointment, the game itself was a bit of a nightmare for our guys. The Waratahs dominated 75 per cent of possession and won 31–3. It was a really bad result from a team perspective, bad from a fan's perspective and bad from an EightyTwenty perspective.

I remember getting home and feeling annoyed, frustrated, angry and embarrassed all at once. It's hard when you are not playing, because you feel helpless to some extent on game day. I was disappointed for the guys, but I felt even more miserable about the whole charity thing. Perhaps it was bad timing after all the natural disasters that had occurred in the early part of 2011. Had people's charity quota been dried up by already helping Queensland flood and Christchurch earthquake victims?

I just felt so down about it all. I was humbled by how much the general admission ticketholders had donated, more than we ever thought we'd get from the collection buckets, but the corporate side of things had been a bit of a lead balloon. I took it personally because I already felt really uncomfortable asking for money. I still didn't want people to think I was always asking for money and I don't want to become a 'bleeding heart', as my grandfather says. I want everyone to see the people of Nkayi (and millions of other people like them) not as victims, but as amazing people who want to get themselves out of the situation they are in. The reason we privileged people are able to enjoy the lifestyle we have is because it helps maintain the cycle of imbalance that others, like those in Nkayi, are trying to escape from. I really had to move on from my frustrations, because being angry would solve nothing, so I tried to channel my energy into making me more determined to see EightyTwenty Vision succeed in other ways. I had to let my disappointment go and turn my focus back to my knee rehabilitation.

One week later, on 19 April, I was officially back from injury. I had such a great time at training. I was allowed to participate in most of the drills apart from the heavy contact stuff. It was so good to be part of the squad again—you get to add your energy to the group and feed off their energy. I really enjoyed it.

For the first half of April I did three lower body weights sessions a week, mostly modified lifts at sub-max weights, just trying to get the knee back into it, building strength and my confidence that the ligament had healed. I was getting close to being ready to play again, but was not quite there. I was also doing five or six upper body weights sessions a week, plus a session on the trampoline four days a week, balance/proprioception exercises daily, as well as daily physio for knee mobility and loosening of the muscles around the knee. It was really busy, but my knee started feeling a lot better and my running was getting better too. Most pleasing of all was that the physios and strength and conditioning guys were happy with the GPS data from my running sessions and things were all heading in the right direction.

Just as I was starting to enjoy being back in training with the squad, we had what is now known as a Physical Improvement Day. It used to be called our day off, but the new name reflects a bit of how we're slowly trying to change things at the Force, fostering a culture of guys wanting to improve themselves. I went in and did a bit of weights, and was meant to do a swimming and pool running session as a bit of a top-up, but my groin felt a bit sore. I iced it as a precaution and saw the academy physio to have it checked out. It turned out to be nothing too serious.

It was time to ease off a little on the training front though, so I took to the back garden again in some of the rare spare time I had. I started paving the area out the back where there used to be a spa. It was a really good spa, but Emma and I decided that it was silly having a spa when we lived close to the beach. It used up too much power and water, and we could sell it to fund other projects around the house and use the space better.

I've never paved before and neither had Luke, who offered to help—a decision he probably regretted later on. It seemed easy enough. Get it level and lay pavers—'It's not rocket scientist!' (an often joked-about, mis-quote that came out of the mouth of one of our front rowers at the Force when he got worked up about a lack of understanding during a scrum session).

The paving turned into quite an epic undertaking. We hired a compacter and paver saw, figuring we would knock it off in one day. But it proved a lot harder than we had anticipated. We did get the hang of it and were on a roll, thinking we would be on schedule to almost finish it in a day, but then we ran out of pavers. We had been using pavers from a big pile I found behind the shed and others that I had pulled out to create garden beds. I had miscalculated how many we'd need (or had just assumed that there would be enough). No drama, I thought. I asked Em to head to the local tip to see if there were another 50 or so pavers. They didn't have any. So she went to three other big trade/paver places without any luck—apparently the pavers we were after weren't made anymore.

That was on the Sunday. The next day was the day that we had to make a plan. *Die boere maak plan*—Afrikaans for 'the farmer makes a plan'. Despite not being Afrikaans or speaking the language, my dad would always say this. My family were arriving on Thursday night for Easter and I was determined to have the paving done. Every time my brother Mike comes over it seems like we have just been waiting for him to come to help fix something or build something around the house. That is somewhat true, as he is the handiest handyman I know and I love spending time with him doing projects and chatting, but this time I wanted to show him what I had done, and that I could actually do a project around the house without his help.

Eventually we found some much larger pavers that were the same depth as the other ones we'd used. We managed to get twenty of them and we lay them in the middle before putting a border around the big pavers with the ones we already had. It actually ended up looking quite nice and Mike and the family were suitably impressed. I have marvelled at a few paving jobs I've walked over since then, with a whole new appreciation for how the professionals get them so flat and even.

My comeback from injury was on track through the last half of April, but my return to playing had to wait another week after I pulled up a little bit sore after a running session. I was keen to get back but knew I needed to get myself right first as I was no good to anyone if I wasn't confident out on the field or if I re-injured my knee.

I had been asked to give a speech and present some awards at a ceremony run by one of the local city councils, so headed to that after training. One of the things they asked me to talk about was the challenges I have faced in sport. I talked about injury and how frustrating it was. I spoke about how I had struggled to deal with not being able to play, but I was working on getting better at using the time off to work on other parts of my game. While I have become a lot better at being injured, I still remember my school-boy injury and how I struggled being off the field. My family has some hilarious stories about just how impossible I was at times and Steve often jokes about how I would plead with him to help me practise my passing in the garden and then say, 'Just two hundred passes.'

My first game back from injury finally came at the end of April against the Crusaders in Perth. You never feel 100 per cent after an injury, you just have to have the confidence that you've done all the right things when looking after the injury and hope it will withstand contact in a game. Our medical team are great and they were confident so I was pretty excited about getting back out there. Maintaining match fitness with a lower limb injury is pretty difficult, but I worked really hard in the pool and on the grinder, doing boxing sessions and upper body circuits. However, you have to resign yourself to the fact that you are always going to be underdone, and just deal with the lack of match fitness. It's such a big step up from individual rehab training, which is mainly just straight line running, which then progresses to include swerving and change of direction, to full contact training. Then it's an even bigger step up to playing a full eighty minutes. You might be fine hitting someone holding a hit shield, but going into a ruck, getting on the ball, and being cleaned out then having to get up back into the defensive line and chase a kick, make a tackle or run the ball up is a whole different story.

I was relieved to make it through my comeback match against the Crusaders. It ended in a loss though despite a pretty good comeback from us after Israel Dagg scored two tries for them in the first ten minutes. We were chasing the game after that and the Crusaders held on.

Emma had decided that she would start making me a 'treat' after home games and for this one she baked me a lemon meringue pie. She is always so excited about it, knowing that after a game I'm happy to eat almost anything. On of the things Canno taught me when I first came over to the Force was that you have to treat yourself after a game, so I generally do, as I don't usually have much of an appetite on game day, so am pretty hungry afterwards. After my injury Em had to put her baking plans on hold for a while, but she was back with a vengeance after that game. Not only did she bake me a lemon meringue pie, she brought it in the car and between the game and the post-match function we went to the car for a bit of clandestine pie eating. I found out later that on their way to the post-match James O'Connor and Ben

Whittaker bumped into Em in the car park and tried to take a photo of the pie, so it wasn't as clandestine as I'd hoped. Emma is an amazing cook, and I keep telling her she should do an athlete cookbook, or a cookbook about making healthy meals that are still delicious.

I'm not saying that lemon meringue pie is healthy! It is not. But it's the perfect once-in-a-blue-moon (or home-match) treat. And it was the best lemon meringue pie I've ever eaten—and I'm not just saying that because we're married.

# 10.
# Creating Heroes
### Back to Super Rugby and the birth of Heroes

My return from injury at the end of April was a relief. Coming back the way I did, without much game simulation fitness to give my knee as much time to heal as possible, it took a good few weeks to get my match fitness back and feel like I was having an impact in games. There seemed to be our fair share of hiccups along the way too, with Emma and I both catching a stomach bug in early May. One day, after a full day of training, things had got heated during the field session in the afternoon. This happens every now and then in rugby teams. After the session, we were practising our lineouts for the week and Brownie and Nathan 'Sharpie' Sharpe had a fair disagreement about one aspect of the lineouts for the week and voiced their frustrations. The disagreement was eventually resolved during the session but after training Brownie headed straight for his car. I caught up with him to see if he was ok, but he just wanted to get home and didn't want to chat. Once I got home, I didn't think too much about it. Emma spent that night vomiting and I also didn't manage to get much sleep with the same bug, so I decided to turn my alarm clock off and just sleep in as much as I could. The next day was free of training so I was keen to try and sleep off whatever I had caught. However, instead of sleeping in, we were woken by banging on our door. I tried to block the noise out and Em got up and opened the front door.

Richard Brown burst in at his happy best. I sat up in bed as he came into the room. He wanted to apologise for being short with me after training. I accepted his apology and said that it was not an issue at all. With that, he was off and out the front door before firing up 'Smokey' and pulling out of the driveway. Standard Richard Brown behaviour.

I got my first chance of 2011 to travel with the Force for Super Rugby when we went across to play the Waratahs in Sydney during early May. It was nice to get my first taste of my home-away-from-home for the year—the Crowne Plaza hotel at Coogee. Being at the hotel meant I was playing rugby and I have many fond memories from there. I also have some less than fond ones, including being drug tested for the very first time as a seventeen-year-old. I was in one of the hotel room toilets with the team doctor (who had to be there because I was under eighteen) and the drug tester watching me try to wee into the collection container with my pants down and t-shirt held above my nipples—my first experience of major stage fright. I don't think I've taken that long to wee, before or since. My first camp with the Wallabies was also in Coogee and that was when I found out what it was like to train and live with the Wallabies. I hadn't stayed in Coogee since October 2010 but I walked in and was handed my room key with a friendly 'Welcome back Mr Pocock'.

I have spent so much time there in the past few years, and know the area and the staff at the hotel quite well. And like a lot of the other guys, know the room service menu off by heart too. Almost all our Wallabies camps are based in Coogee. We sometimes have a day or two off between camps, but it's not really worth me flying back to Perth for thirty hours or so, so I end up staying at the hotel a bit longer than most others in the squad. On good days it's great just to hang out at Coogee beach and it's really easy to catch a bus into the city to have a look around. Em's spent so much time there that she made friends with one of the girls who worked at the front desk and was very sad to see her leave recently for a different career.

For the past two years I haven't unpacked my bag from the first Wallabies camp after the Super Rugby season till the end of Spring Tour in December. There is just not long enough in one place so it seems silly to unpack when you get home for two or three days. And there is never space in hotels to unpack when you are sharing rooms— it's easier just to keep it in your bag. I don't mind it too much, but by the end of Spring Tour unpacking my bag and sleeping in my own bed are fairly high on the priority list.

Our game against the Waratahs ended up being a tough loss to take. It was only my second match back from injury and we managed to grind out the first half well to be leading 9–7 at half-time, with the Waratahs' try coming from a penalty kick that hit the crossbar before rebounding into the arms of our former teammate Ryan Cross, who strolled over, so we were unlucky not to have a better lead. Then in the second half we were leading 15–13 with only ten minutes to go, but the Waratahs crossed for a late converted try to steal the match.

After a loss like that you just want to get back out on the field as quickly as you can to make amends, but our second bye of the season fell on the following weekend and we had to wait two weeks for another chance. Part of me was actually looking forward to this particular bye though, because Em and I were expecting the Noffs to come and stay so we could brainstorm more ideas around the ethical boot concept, although we were aware it would take years to get to the market and start using the proceeds for EightyTwenty Vision. It was also the weekend of my Force teammate Matt Hodgson's wedding.

Training over our bye weekend was classified as 'unsupervised active rest', which basically means we had to sort ourselves out and just do a bit of gym and/or cardio each day, and were only given a program if we thought we needed one. On the Friday, Em and I went to Reabold Hill in Perth and did a hills session the Force trainer had put together for us. We had not run together since our honeymoon, so it was quite fun. It was all timed stuff, thirty seconds flat out up the hill with a jog back recovery, so we could just run at our own pace. Then we went home and I finally got to oil the table Mike and I built a few weeks before when he'd visited for the Easter weekend. Yes, I did manage to get the pavers all sorted for them in time, but it wouldn't have been a complete visit for Mike if he hadn't helped us with something handy. He and I made the table using the timber from the decking that was around the spa we had pulled out, and it was looking amazing. In truth, I had come up with the idea and had a rough plan of a table with benches. But Mike made it a reality while I was at training and I helped out when I got home. We had already used the table quite a bit by that stage, but I wanted to give it a coat of oil to weatherproof it and ensure the timber wouldn't crack or age too quickly.

In the afternoon, we ducked out to the airport to pick up Matt and Naomi Noffs with their daughter Amelie. Their plane was delayed fifteen minutes, which, unfortunately, put all of our plans out for the afternoon and we were a quarter of an hour late to Matt Hodgson and Jodi Grubb's wedding. I felt a bit bad because by the time we pulled into the car park they were out by the river having their photos taken, Em and I had missed the ceremony. The reception was great, though I did feel a bit sorry for Matt, who had asked friends who had known him for a bit too long to MC and give speeches, resulting in some merciless shaming.

For the remainder of the weekend, Em, Luke, Bec and myself spent lots of time picking Matt and Naomi Noffs's brains about the boot concept, while being thoroughly entertained by their 10-month-old daughter Amelie. Matt and Naomi have a unique style of parenting, which makes Amelie a content and confident baby. She's so sure of their care that she hardly cries at all. It was really interesting for Em and I to witness. Matt and Naomi have purposely tried to limit baby-related consumption and make do with very minimal baby accessories.

Naomi has spent a lot of time in developing countries and says that if those women can do it with so few resources, surely we don't need as much as we seem to think we do.

In my own experience, asking mothers in a hospital in Zimbabwe who were less than a week away from giving birth, 'What do you need to make it easier for you at the hospital?', it was almost comical when their measured reply was that they would love a few netballs to play with and keep them 'fit'. The hospital they were at had no electricity or running water and they had to provide and cook their own food, so you would think these women may like something more than a netball. But their experience of motherhood is so far removed from ours and while they lack many resources they are so capable with the few resources they have. Nae and Matt's understanding that we can learn a lot from women in these places was such a good reminder for Em and me.

Among all the boot talk with the Noffs, we spent a bit of time at the beach paddle boarding and half a day down in Fremantle looking around the markets and lunching at Little Creatures. The weekend really served as a great time for us to get to know the Noffs better and move forward with our plans. The concept became known tentatively as 'Heroes Boots'. The idea behind it was that anyone can be a hero by choosing to buy products that give all the people in the production chain a fair share of the pie. The design process began and a final design was sent off a couple of weeks later so a prototype could be created for us to have a look at.

The process was quite daunting and we tried to learn as much as we could in a short space of time to ensure we were making the right decisions. I had been researching the sports apparel industry for a few years and had taken to blanking out the logos on my boots, too embarrassed to wear footwear that was likely made by someone working in poor conditions, for very little. I remember walking through a big sports store over in New Zealand during the latter part of the Super

Rugby season, looking at all the boots on display, trying to figure out how an ethical boot would even fit into the market. I was not a boot designer but I didn't want to be wearing boots that were made for less than a cup of coffee and I wanted to create options for people who felt the same. The boots in the sports store in NZ had all sorts of fancy gimmicks to apparently make you run faster, step better, kick further. The word 'technology' seemed to come up a lot.

At the end of the day, surely you just want comfort, grip and quality in a boot, don't you? Well, that's all I really wanted. Players who get paid money to wear boots, don't play as well as they do because they wear a certain boot—they probably wear that particular boot because they get paid to and they get paid to wear it because they are very good at what they do.

Creating Heroes Boots was also daunting because it has not really been done before. Do people really care about the ethics of where their things are made? Are people willing to change the way they buy so that other people who they will never know might have a life that is free from poverty? And how do we create a quality boot that holds its own against others? If we are going to do this it has to be, first and foremost, a good boot and the ethical side of it just backs this up as a foundation of our business.

Luke did some market research and created a business plan, while he and I both looked at possible start-up capital and how we could raise it. I believe in the goodness of human nature. There are a lot of bad things happening in the world, but deep down I believe we are good. Call me naive or idealistic, but I really believe that once people become more educated and there is more public debate and pressure around issues like child slavery, then the proliferation of sweatshops, poor wages, and the lack of freedom to form unions in the clothing industry, these will become things of the past. We can vote with our wallets, and companies will change when they can't sell their products. It is surely just a matter of time, and a big part of this is giving consumers an alternative, which we hope to do.

After the Noffs visit, Luke and I had a meeting with a guy who said his accounting firm could help EightyTwenty Vision with its accounting and books. It has been something that we've been talking about for some time: with me playing rugby, there had been very little time to devote to the business side of things.

Luke was staying up late doing the accounting as well as working and being a dad, so it was a timely offer and the guy seemed genuine with very little agenda around getting involved. He just wanted to help out, which was very refreshing. After meeting him a few times we soon realised what an amazing person he is, with a great heart and is keen to support what we are doing. This new addition to our ranks has helped us immensely and allowed Luke and I to devote more time to improving the project on the ground in Nkayi while raising more funds across Australia.

May 2011 eventually turned out to be a really good month for all things EightyTwenty. Momentum continued through June as we started to get some more publicity. One of the more enjoyable interviews I had the pleasure of doing was with Lindsay 'The Doctor' McDougall, from Triple J's afternoon program during what was a very busy 'day off' from Force training duties.

A few weeks earlier, James O'Connor had come to me and said he'd been asked to do a segment called 'The Secret Skills of Athletes' with 'some guy from Triple J'. I was immediately both excited and disappointed. As an avid Triple J listener, who listens to 'The Doctor' most days on my way home from training, I admit that I felt pretty cheated when James was asked because I know that he rarely, if ever, would listen to Triple J. Of course, in hindsight that's pretty silly—I get asked to do interviews all the time for stations I don't ever listen to, so it was rather hypocritcal of me.

After a few weeks of Triple J not being able to tee up an interview time with James, one of the media people at the Force mentioned it to me and was probably a little surprised by the enthusiasm of my response. Of course I would do the interview, but it then meant I was under the pump to think of a 'secret skill'.

Dave 'The Wolfman' Williams, of rugby league fame with Manly, had pumped up the hype on a craze known as 'planking'—which eventually turned out to be a reckless and sometimes deadly act (but which was in no way Dave's fault)—by proclaiming it as his 'secret skill' on Triple J. I had listened to his segment and it was really funny. I didn't really have a cool 'skill' like that, so in the end, I decided to acknowledge my love of arts and crafts. It may come as a surprise, but I love painting, screen printing and collaging, although I draw a definite line at scrapbooking. I'd say it would have to be some sort of cardinal sin to scrapbook, but apart from that I'm usually up for a good old 'craftanoon'.

The interview was on our day off in the morning. Following my interview at Triple J, I headed straight to a lunch at the Oxford. Some Force fans, who had won a competition, were receiving playing jerseys and getting to have lunch with the player of their choice. So Sharpie and I ended up having lunch at the Oxford with four people—a couple who are heavily involved with local rugby in Perth, and a father and son.

After that I headed home to meet Em and then had an interview with Channel 9 for a couple of hours. Tim Sheridan from the *Wide World of Sports* was putting together a few features on some of the Wallaby hopefuls for the Rugby World Cup. He had already interviewed Mum and Dad at home in Brisbane and he wanted to interview me and then Em and I together.

It's sometimes overwhelming when your 'day off' gets filled with so much stuff, and that day came during what had been a pretty busy week. Throughout June I was becoming increasingly aware of how little time we had left in Perth before Wallabies commitments kicked in, so I tried to get on top of EightyTwenty work as much as I could, plus sort out all of our personal medical/tax/finance for the end of the financial year.

I guess a lot of people would see the life of a rugby player as being very glamorous and luxurious and, in a lot of ways, it is. We are reasonably well paid, we get to travel the world, and often have access to things and experiences that others do not. This all comes at a cost though. There is obviously a pretty huge physical toll, but there is also the cost of a lot of your personal freedom. There is not really any room to negotiate our schedules. And we are 'owned' in some ways by our Super Rugby franchise and the ARU. This means that everything else has to come secondary to our work. We can't get time off for many things at all. We miss lots of weddings, birthdays, births, funerals and, with a few exceptions, we can do very little about it.

This has never really been a particularly big problem for me, because I lived away from my family and, before Em, I never really even had a serious girlfriend. That is, apart from when I was at school and the first six months or so of living in Perth when I dated a girl called Laura. She was the first girl I could ever talk to and relate to and have fun with. But living so far away and being so preoccupied with training weren't the best conditions for a relationship and it ended. So with Em there were a lot of big learning curves. It's been different over the last two years though. I've reconsidered the many times I scoffed at the other guys when they were lamenting being away from their partners, or when I thought poorly of their wives/girlfriends who seemed to complain about being apart. Now I realise it wasn't weakness on their part, but rather the difficulties of trying to be in a healthy relationship while playing professional rugby. Fortunately Em and I have managed to work out some pretty good ways to work things through and sort out any conflicts, so that we're able to deal with it when we're finding it hard. Em has also taken 2011 off work so she can travel with me more and we'll actually get to spend time together.

The preliminary Wallabies schedule was released in June and, provided I was selected for all of the squads and was injury-free, it looked like between July and mid-November 2011 I would not get home at all, unless I headed back to Perth for two days—which means you lose half the time travelling. So it's fortunate for us that we're in a position where Em is not forced to work and has the freedom (and inclination) to travel with me.

It hasn't been without its struggles for Em though. As a feminist she initially struggled with feeling as though her life was revolving around me and my work, but having more free time has allowed her to flourish in lots of ways—spending lots of time gardening, blogging and helping out with emails when I was busy, as well as learning how to do tax and budget stuff. Learning how to do a tax return was definitely a new experience. She also came to the realisation that whether or not she works isn't what makes her a 'good feminist', for want of a better expression.

We had two games in New Zealand before heading back to Australia for our last two games of the Super Rugby season. We played the Hurricanes in Palmerston North, my first time in the place. I wasn't too sure what to expect because a Wellington businessman I had spoken to had seemed somewhat exasperated: 'Palmerston North? What the hell are they doing sending you fellas out there to play?'

Such are the opinions of big citydwellers I guess—I quite liked the place. I often have a chuckle when people belittle some of the smaller towns on the Super Rugby circuit—Perth even cops it sometimes. I imagine if people could see the town where I went to school in Gweru, Zimbabwe, they would have a good laugh and have something negative to say about it. There was not a lot to keep a city-slicker occupied, but I guess you make your own fun and there's something wrong if you need to walk around a shopping centre to keep you occupied.

The match against the Hurricanes was always going to be tough after a number of injuries to our inside backs, leaving behind James

O'Connor, Brett Sheehan, Willie Ripia and Gene Fairbanks. The backline was reshuffled with a few new faces added. It ended up being one of those games when you probably aren't expected to do well, but have a real dig. James Stannard was great, filling in at flyhalf, and we scored a few good team tries. Our defence was generally a lot better than weeks gone by, but a few lapses allowed the Hurricanes to score and we went down by a try. We were bitterly disappointed as it was a huge team effort given the number of injuries and we had done enough to win. A highlight was Ben McCalman getting his first try for the club—a long time coming, so he thought.

Our doctor has been trying to get one of the boys in the team to read a book. A lot of the guys take a book to read during travel at airports, on the bus or aeroplane, but this outside back (yes, not a front rower) claims to have not read a book except the ones he was forced to read at school. It was an entertaining spectacle, the two of them trying to choose a book at the airport bookshop.

'Doc, I need something that's interesting and easy to read', he said as he picked up a Richard Dawkins' book.

The Doc replied: 'He's a brilliant author but that should definitely not be your first book.'

Due to a lack of choice they eventually settled on *A Brief History of Everything* by Ken Wilber. A few hours later the doc asked the player how he'd gone making a start at reading the book.

'Doc, I read the first page but there were heaps of words I didn't understand and I was tired so I went to sleep', the player replied.

'Not to worry', the Doc said. 'In Dunedin we'll find you an easier book to read, a book that's written in the vernacular.'

I burst out laughing. I love our team banter when we travel—it's great that we have such a wide collection of different personalities in the mix.

The team pulled together really well after the narrow loss to the Hurricanes. We posted a solid win against the Highlanders in Dunedin during the second week of our New Zealand mini tour. The victory actually did the Waratahs a few favours for a play-off position, as it effectively ended the Highlanders' hopes, so I guess it was good to be helping another Australian franchise in a Rugby World Cup year. We've had a fairly decent record against the Highlanders so it was great to beat them in our last game at the 'House of Pain', Carisbrook, in Dunedin. Post-Rugby World Cup, they are moving to the new state-of-the-art indoor Otago Stadium.

As the Super Rugby season drew to a close, we were out of finals contention but it didn't change the way we approached our games and we put in some good performances. Our two last matches were against the competition leaders, Queensland Reds at home in Perth, and then Melbourne Rebels away. The Reds match showed us why they were leading the competition, beating us in the final minutes despite us dominating most of the match. We lost Sharpie early on and I was handed the captaincy for the remainder of the match. I also managed to cross for a try, so that was nice, but I would have swapped it straight away for a better team result in the end. The guys played really well and it was so disappointing to lose in the second last minute of play. But to their credit the Reds never gave up and they scraped through with a victory that eventually had a major bearing on them finishing top of the table. They were a great team and a lot of what they tried seemed to come off, as is the case when you have talented individuals that really believe in their ability.

The inaugural Super 15 season was a great success in terms of the new format, giving fans more local derbies and more matches overall, but we had fairly limited success at the Force. We finished with a victory over the Rebels in Melbourne, but it was another season with a lot of close losses and a few good performances scattered between. Hopefully, we are getting nearer to being on the better side of the ledger in those close games, now that we have had so many to learn from.

Finalising James O'Connor's contract caused quite a bit of disruption in the last weeks of the season—it just seemed to drag out so long. It had reached the point where everyone just wanted the decision to be made so we could move on and finish our season on a high together as a team.

In the final week of the season we cooked breakfast for the Emergency Department staff at Charles Gairdner Hospital. We started cooking just before 6AM, an early start on our day off, but it was the only time that worked with the shift change so that people arriving and leaving for their shifts could all have breakfast. Our team doctor is a trauma specialist at the hospital and the Emergency Department had helped with x-rays, ultrasounds, etc. so much over the years and we could pop in to see the doc or one of his colleagues at any time of the day or night.

James was the only person in the squad who didn't turn up to the breakfast. The boys were filthy and knew something was up. I later found out that the Force were tired of waiting for him to make a decision and had heard from reliable sources that he'd signed in Melbourne, so they put a deadline on him, which was that morning. It turned out no decision was made in time and the Force pulled their offer. Whether or not James's management were just calling the Force's bluff or he had decided on Melbourne is anyone's guess, but he wouldn't be with us next year. It was a sad day. James had joined the Force in 2008, fresh out of school, and we had become good mates playing with the Wallabies and spending much of the year in the same teams. It is disappointing not to have him around in 2012, but this is how it goes in professional sport and I'm sure we'll stay in contact and hopefully play for the Wallabies together for years to come (but you can never take things like playing for the Wallabies for granted).

I have chatted to James quite a bit since it has all blown over and there are always two sides to the story. He missed the breakfast at the hospital because he was at home trying to decide his future, which is totally understandable as he must have been under a fair bit of pressure to decide his future. I think he would have liked to have stayed at the Force had his negotiations gone smoother, but it didn't work out and he is now really excited about starting afresh in Melbourne and being part of hopefully making the Rebels a force in the Super Rugby competition. He is an amazingly talented individual and has applied himself well and I hope he goes on to become an integral part of the Rebels and do really well there.

It was a mix of emotions watching the 2011 Super Rugby final. To be honest I haven't watched many finals since I've started playing for the Force. Being in a competition and not being in the finals doesn't sit well with me. I seem to just get cranky watching it, and inevitably end up going for a run or heading to the gym. The 2011 season was a bit of an exception though, as I followed the Reds' progress in the finals because I have a few good mates in the team—guys I'd played schoolboy and age-group representative rugby with like Quade Cooper, Will Genia, Ben Tapuai, Ben Daley and James Hansen. It was great to see the Reds win the competition and I was hopeful some of their momentum would feed into the Wallabies camp in the weeks that followed.

# 11.
# Wake-up Calls
## Samoa shock and an All Black lesson in Auckland

The extended Wallabies squad assembled on the second Sunday in July 2011, minus the Reds players. They were given a day to take in their Super Rugby triumph before joining us on the Monday. It was a very busy week leading up to the Samoa test, but great to be in the familiar surrounds of a Wallabies camp. It had a particularly special feeling with a World Cup only two months away.

In a way, I feel like I have one set of friends for the first half of the year and then a different set of friends for the second half. I spend the majority of my time with two different groups of people, both of them full of colourful characters.

Luke Burgess is a player I have spent the second half of the year with for the past few seasons. On day one of the 2011 camp, I was treated to some of his finest behaviour when he began to serenade me in the hotel elevator with a made-up song, 'You've gotta release the soul into the bushes. Then go round the back and release the pigeon.'

Burgess is a livewire in the team—he does not seem to have an 'off' switch—and is continually doing things like singing, annoying people or answering questions in team meetings when there is too much of a silence or pause. I get on well with him and really enjoy his company. We have some great chats and he is very passionate about rugby and about improving himself and the team. He will be missed when he heads to France in 2012. Toulouse isn't going to know what's hit them when Luke arrives there after the World Cup campaign.

I spoke with the Wallabies doctor, Warren McDonald, and the physios, James and Andrew, about a niggling injury in my foot that I had picked up towards the end of the Super rugby season after being stood on at training, which lead to the irritation of a tendon. It was inflamed and pretty sore and I had managed it for the last month of the season to get through the games but it had not healed as quickly as was expected.

It was decided, in the lead-up to the Samoa game, that I would rehab run early in the week, with the aim of being up to speed and available to play. However, my hopes were quickly dashed when I was not announced in the team on the Tuesday. It was disappointing—you never want to miss a game for Australia—but at least it gave me an extra week to get my foot right and go into the Tri-Nations with more confidence.

We had our first of a few big injury setbacks during the week before playing Samoa. I was on the sideline talking to Drew Mitchell after we'd finished our rehab when Benn Robinson hobbled over after a drill, telling the physios that he'd 'tweaked' his knee. They put some ice on it and got him back to the hotel to check it out. After an MRI, which showed meniscal damage, he was in for a scope that day and they found damage to his anterior cruciate ligament (ACL), which ruled him out of rugby for the rest of the year.

The first the squad heard of it was at a team meeting later that night when Robbie announced that Robbo was out. There was an audible gasp from the group and I sunk in my chair as I thought about Benn and how much hard work he had put in to get his other injuries right with the Rugby World Cup in his sights.

'Fat cat', as he is affectionately known, has been a big part of the Wallabies for the past few years, with his humour and an all-round nice guy likeability. He's an important part of the squad and has become renowned as one of the best props in world rugby. I love listening to him talk about the pigs he has out on a property in central New South Wales.

In the weeks that followed, Benn had some positive news about his injury. He was apparently part of a unique portion of the population (3 per cent) who are not as reliant on their ACL for running movement. It offered him a glimmer of hope to forgo an operation and return to the squad and play in the Rugby World Cup. But he soon came to realise that it just wasn't right for him and he formally withdrew from the rehab program to have the operation. I felt really sorry for Benn after his World Cup dream was over for 2011, but I have no doubt he will be back to play a big part in the Wallabies in years to come.

Just as the news about Benn had sunk in, on the Friday before the Samoa match there was another injury. James O'Connor, Quade Cooper and Kurtley Beale were appearing for a sponsor in a videotaped session of them running drills, chip kicks and side stepping. It was cold and rainy and the boys had suggested that perhaps it wasn't a good idea since they hadn't warmed up. But they were talked around and James ended up tweaking his hamstring. It ruled him out of the Samoa test.

It's a tough balance, as a player, when you're so responsible for managing your body but you also have many other competing demands—it occasionally doesn't end well. Being ruled out because of something like that was really frustrating for James, but one guy's loss is another's gain and it gave Queensland Reds flyer Rod Davies a starting spot on the wing for his debut.

During our pre-game meeting, Robbie talked about the importance of a good start to the Wallabies 2011 season. He told us that this was no ordinary year and that we had to start the way we wanted to carry on. 'Make a difference to your mates—proactively. When your back is against the wall it's easy, you have to offer a response. We have to be more proactive and make every moment count. It might be too late to wait till our backs are against the wall.'

Sunday was game day—the Wallabies' first game of the year. I ran the water for the team. It was interesting being on the field but not playing. You feel somewhat helpless, like a fly on the wall, but at least you can relay messages from the coaches and give the players feedback about what the coaches are thinking.

Samoa came out hard and defended really well, dishing out the brutal hits they are known for. Their approach was to slow our ball down at the breakdown, and our debutant scrum-half Nick Phipps had a tough time trying to find any space around the ruck. As a result, we never really got into the game in attack and when we finally did, late in the second half, it was too late.

It was like a bad dream. The whole time I kept thinking, 'We'll kick up another gear, and it'll be fine' but it never happened. Samoa recorded a famous victory, much to the delight of their fans. It was far from an ideal start to the year for the Wallabies, but one we would have to live with and improve on.

We had to focus on playing South Africa six days later and the chance to turn our game around against an even more formidable opponent. We had to improve a lot and make the most of the short turnaround amid extensive analysis of what went wrong.

I watched the Samoan game again and, in particular, the breakdown, where we struggled to build momentum through quick ball for our backs. Our supporting players were too slow and this allowed the Samoans to get on the ball and slow it down. We were too high in our clean outs—too many 'shoulders on backs' is the term often used. I had already had a chat to our breakdown coach, David Nucifora, about it and he had talked about a few drills during the week that would be used to correct that problem.

We also needed to have a big focus on staying on our feet against the Springboks. The referee assigned to the match, Chris Pollock, is very hard on the tackler not rolling away and on players arriving at the breakdown leaving their feet, which makes for a great game if you can avoid this. Pollock also takes control of games very early on, setting the tone for the game with players, and it was one of the main points I put up on the weekly referee review board that I had been doing up for the team: 'Very harsh early on but becomes more lenient after the twenty minute mark'. Playing against a goal kicker like Morne Steyn, you cannot afford to give away penalties in your half as these are an almost-certain three points. A few of those and it begins to add up very quickly.

We also reviewed the Samoa game together as a team—Robbie going through some general team stuff, then Phil Blake talking about the defensive side of things and the structures that we needed to stick to, followed by Nucifora pointing out areas to improve at the breakdown. Reviews after losses are never fun, but they are sometimes when you learn the most.

When the team was named for the test against South Africa, there were a few notable changes. Nathan Sharpe was out and the Reds second row (James Horwill and Rob Simmons) in, plus a few other rested Reds players. Pat McCabe was now at inside centre with Matt Giteau not even on the bench. The omission of Gits was obviously big news for the media and they were quick to pounce on it and speculate as to the reasons. I was disappointed for Matt but pretty excited for Pat, who has worked very hard to get where he has since we played in the same Australian Schoolboys team back in 2005.

I loved playing with Matt at the Force and the Wallabies. He has proven himself over a long period of time with over ninety Test caps. A few people who don't know Gits personally think he is arrogant and self-absorbed, but it's just not the case—he is a genuine team player who works hard and, despite his quirkiness, he puts the team first around selection and in games. It's this self-assurance and confidence that rubs off on the players around him and often make him the centre of conversation or joke-telling in a group.

Robbie ended the team meeting by talking about how it was now a 'four game campaign'. We were not looking any further than that. We wanted to win the Tri-Nations, but, as he put it bluntly, 'We haven't won because we haven't deserved it. It's up to us to become deserving.' We all knew his words were true—we had improved and fought hard, yet hadn't been the most deserving. But we had the opportunity to change that.

The Wednesday before the Springboks clash in July was our first 'day off' since we came into camp and I managed to cram a fair bit in. I headed down the road to do some weights with Ben McCalman a bit earlier than the rest of the squad, as we were both invited to a corporate lunch and didn't want to be late for it. I had met one of the organisers last year and she had generously given me the opportunity to talk about EightyTwenty Vision. Phil Kearns was MC and he was going to share some thoughts about the Humpty Dumpty Foundation that he is involved with. It does an amazing job fundraising to provide healthcare equipment for paediatric services. George Gregan was also there giving some insight into his last few years of rugby in Japan and the George Gregan Foundation's work building playgrounds at hospitals around Australia.

I remember George running a coaching clinic at Churchie in Brisbane in 2003 that I had attended. I had loved it and had been a big fan; I even played against him in 2007. I was actually busy reading George's autobiography at that time and was a bit bummed when I forgot to take it to the lunch to get it signed by him.

The lunch went well and I met some really nice people, but I couldn't stay around too long after it. I had an appointment that afternoon at Gideon Shoes to talk to two guys who help with brand development. They had recently come on board at Gideon and wanted to talk with Luke and me (Luke via conference call from Perth) about what we were doing with Heroes Boots and ways that they could add value. It sounded really promising and it was good to keep the whole concept moving.

The Wallabies were quickly back into training on the Thursday and, despite all the rain, our morning session was one of the better ones since we had assembled. In the week leading up to the Springboks game, Sydney had more rain than it usually did for the entire month of July. A lot of the fields were closed, but we managed to get on to Sydney Grammar School. It resembled more of a swamp, with puddles covering much of the field and rain bucketing down the entire session. I thought it was a lot of fun. A few of the backs tiptoed onto the field a bit gingerly with their skins and wet weather jackets with hoods to try and stay dry, but it was futile. By the end of the session everyone was soaked.

The weather didn't give up and the stadium was unavailable for our captain's run because it was too wet, and there was a rugby league match to be played on it that night. The captain's run was moved to St Joseph's College at Hunters Hill, where returning old boy Kurtley Beale was a big hit with a few of the students who came down to watch us train even though it absolutely poured the entire time. The team was switched on and ready to go. Despite the conditions, it ended up being a sharp run with very little dropped ball.

The nerves were now kicking in. It was the first Test match of the year for me and there's a big step up from Super Rugby to Test matches in terms of build-up and expectation. Even without reading any newspapers, you just know how many people feel the same and want the team to do well. It wasn't long ago that I was one of those kids whose emotions mirrored how well the Wallabies played on a Saturday night.

Nerves are something that every player has to deal with and players suffer from them to varying degrees. Some guys don't seem to be affected at all, but when I start to feel nervous I know I am ready for the game. It's also hard, sometimes, before games because you want to see friends and family, but you are not always great company on game day. Em and I have developed a fairly good routine when we're together. We hang out a bit and I try not to get too grumpy and she knows not to make too much fun of me.

Em had flown in from Perth on the Thursday before the match, so we could spend game day together. The night before a Test we all have to sleep at the team hotel. This ensures we get a good night's sleep. Em was staying at a hotel down the road, so when I woke up at about 7AM I went down to her hotel and slept for another few hours. I usually try to have a really good sleep on game day (sometimes Em gets impatient and goes out for a run while I'm asleep) and then we usually go for a walk or for a swim in the ocean, but that wasn't an option on this day with Coogee posting pretty dangerous swell.

Instead we walked down the road to this great little cafe and had a bit of lunch. After that I went back to the hotel to have a nap while Em went off to buy some wellington boots. Having grown up in Port Hedland, in north-west Western Australia, she still isn't used to the cold and wet. Sydney had more rain than she'd ever seen before (even in a cyclone), so she was in awe of the amount of water she was seeing.

You could sense the excitement in the group as kick-off drew nearer. Robbie addressed us before we got onto the bus. He emphasised the fact that a win would keep all options open and put us in a position to win the Tri-Nations. We headed out to the stadium knowing that it would take a huge step up from the previous performance against Samoa to match it with South Africa.

We dominated early and our backs made in-roads into their defence. Will Genia caused havoc down the blindside, running at their front rowers and Stephen Moore ran a superb line in the midfield to cut through and score a try, even putting a little step on the fullback to get over the line. Ben Alexander then capped off a good team try on the wing. He copped a bit from the group after the game for getting the ball off Rocky to score, pretty much blocking Digby Ioane out of the play. Ben loves a try and seems to sniff them out more than most front rowers, so you know when you're near the line he is always going to have a crack.

It was great to bounce back with a victory over the Springboks following the shock loss to Samoa. Will, Rocky, Robbie and I went to the post-match press conference. It was my first one for the year with the Wallabies. For most of it I sat there thinking (and having a bit of a chuckle) about our old team doctor at the Force, Mark de Cruz, saying that even after a win press conferences are so boring because no one ever smiles. It's like you can't be happy about the win because you have to say the right things about preparing for next week. Mark is always making sure I enjoy my rugby while it lasts and never take it for granted.

The victory put us in a good frame of mind for the next ten days, which were spent in a training camp at The Southport School (TSS) on the Gold Coast. There were definitely positives to take out of the game against South Africa, but we all knew they were pretty average in the game, and had left a lot of their regular squad back in South Africa to rehab and train after the Super Rugby season. We knew very well that while we counter-attacked well and scored a few good tries, we still had a long way to go if we were going to achieve what we wanted to in 2011.

We had the usual Monday afternoon flush session—nothing too hard. A few pass races and skill games with a few local schoolboys. It's great to give a few kids the opportunity to train with us, and while it's not a proper full session as such, it must still be a buzz for them. I can imagine how excited I would have been to have that opportunity. I remember once sneaking out of class to go and watch Ireland train on the Churchie school ovals.

After dinner on the first night at TSS we had a presentation with Blackberry, a Wallabies sponsor. We were all given a phone and we were supposed to be using them, so they were giving us a rundown of how to get the most out of the phone. The guy from Blackberry had his phone hooked up to a projector and was running through some of the features. He started to talk about Twitter and his stream came up on the screen. As a bit of a rugby fan he was following all the boys who were on Twitter. Quade seized the opportunity and quickly tweeted, 'In the most boring meeting ever', which came up on the screen to roars of laughter from the group. Luckily the presenter saw the funny side and quickly quipped, 'Mate, you could have at least tweeted from your Blackberry' as it came up 'via Twitter for iPhone'.

That first week of the camp at TSS was really busy, but also very enjoyable. Nathan Sharpe is an old boy at the school and no doubt still revered among the students. He was very at home in the facilities, although there's no doubt they are very different since the big guy was there almost fifteen years ago. Sharpie had his boys there one day at the pool and it was great to see them.

Partners and family were encouraged to join us at Southport, but not too many of the guys had kids—it is really just Sharpie, Salesi Ma'afu, Sekope Kepu, Pek Cowan, Radike Samo and Mark Gerrard. Most of the professional support staff had families though, and lots of them came up for the weekend. Penny Deans, Robbie's wife, offered her support and local knowledge to the partners and parents who were preparing to head over to New Zealand for the Rugby World Cup, which was very helpful.

After a solid week of training, we had the weekend off, so Em and I made our way up to Brisbane for a couple of days off. We stopped in at my favourite cafe in West End, BlackStar, for a bit of dinner. The owners, Marty and Vonnie, happened to be there so they had some dinner with us. I always make a point of going to BlackStar when I'm in Brisbane. It's easily my favourite cafe in the world. Marty roasts the beans himself and sells them to a number of other cafes around the city, where they're distributed by bicycle throughout the CBD. He's experimenting with various kinds of fair-trade coffee, trying to be committed to both excellent coffee and uncompromising ethics.

The weekend off was still very busy. Saturday morning I had two photo shoots before heading to watch the Churchie Under-14s, which my brother Steve had coached that year. They were playing Toowoomba Grammar School in the last game of the season. The head of rugby at Churchie pulled me aside and asked me if I'd speak to the First XV and wish them luck, so I did and it brought back some fond memories.

Em and I spent the afternoon catching up with some friends and I watched the All Blacks play the Springboks with Dad. We rarely get a chance to watch rugby together anymore, so it was nice to sit there and share our thoughts about various players and debate aspects of play.

My dad is my hero. When I grew up, he was everything I wanted to become and from my teenage years I respected him greatly for what he had done for our family and how hard he worked. Moving away from home as a seventeen-year-old I missed out on a bit and have to make the most of a predominately long-distance relationship with my family. Steve lived with me in Perth for four months before hurting his back and returning to Brisbane to pursue his university studies. I had been pretty focused about rugby at school and Steve had been working through issues of his own.

Mum is the one to hold our family together. She is such an amazing mother and friend. She encouraged us to each become our own person and not to feel that we need to follow the crowd or fulfil specific roles. She can be fairly feisty at times, and you know that if Mum is pushed too far there will be trouble. Emma and my mother are best of friends now and Dad always jokingly complains that Em is radicalising Mum's views, but I think it has been great for my mum to have another woman in our male-dominated family.

Our time in Brisbane went really fast and before I knew it we were back at TSS on the Sunday, ready for a big week leading up to the clash against the All Blacks in Auckland. I was excited and it was great because we could start fresh. In a normal week after a weekend game

I'm usually very sore till Tuesday, so I don't get a great deal done, but that week we had an ideal run after the weekend off.

Everyone looked refreshed and the sessions in that second week at TSS leading up to the All Blacks game were really sharp and focused. Will Genia and Quade Cooper have noticeably improved their communication and direction around the field and it is a lot easier to play with a halves combination that gives early and clear calls.

Sometimes it seems a few of us are too eager. The coaching staff ended up putting time limits on weights sessions and not allowing us to do extra top-up running sessions after training. As a player you just have to trust that the strength and conditioning coach has it all planned out. We wear GPS devices and heart rate monitors for every field session so they can monitor the amount of work we're getting through and make sure we are doing enough running in our legs, but not too much. The majority of guys are keen to train and want to get really stuck into it, but we trust our trainers and stick to the plan in the hope that, come game day on the weekend, we are all fresh and ready to rip in.

We arrived in Auckland at midnight. The flight over wasn't the most comfortable. I was in a window seat next to Ben McCalman, who is not the smallest bloke, and he was next to Patricio Noriega, who is a man-mountain. I did enjoy a good chat with Ben, though, about farming and all sorts of other things.

The first press conference in Auckland was pretty entertaining. The day before, Steve Hanson, the All Blacks forwards coach, had said that the Wallabies didn't respect the All Blacks. I actually had no idea this had happened until our media manager Matt McIlraith prepped us on it before the press conference. It seemed a strange thing to say and it didn't fuss any of us. We laughed it off and decided to do the same in the press conference, as there was no reason to give the All Blacks any extra fuel for the game. The questions came thick and hard at Robbie about the Hanson statement. There were about thirty people in the room from the various media outlets. After five or so questions they seemed to bore of trying to get a good angle on that before getting stuck on the Hong Kong game in 2010 when we won. After another spate of questions, Robbie asked one journo, 'Please, can we maybe talk about things that have happened this year? Hong Kong was ages ago.'

There is a sports news program on New Zealand television that doesn't take itself too seriously and finds a humorous angle on things. Quite a few boys actually enjoy watching the show when we are over there—it's more a Roy and H.G. kind of approach to things. The first question one of these guys asked me was, 'David, you have an interesting surname. Do you know what it means?' I thought it was pretty funny and had a good chuckle before telling him I had no idea and that Google was probably his best bet.

He wasn't finished though: 'And David, how did you manage to smuggle those pythons in through customs last night?' I had no idea what he was talking about, until he started pointing towards his biceps and then I clicked. I explained how much quicker the Rugby World Cup arrivals process was (which they were trialling on us as a team), and how I had experienced no trouble getting the 'pythons' through customs.

The same TV program crept up unexpectedly again after the captain's run the following day. In the change room after the run, Luke Burgess was up to his usual antics, dancing away in his undies. No one saw a camera peeking through the glass window in the change room door and they got it all. It was the same mob who had asked me those questions at the press conference. Luke featured in their program that night.

There was another funny moment for the group after the captain's run, when Anthony Faingaa was tweeting and asked James Horwill how you spell Dunedin. He was about to tweet 'Just finished captain's run—Dunedin Stadium is a great venue,' when someone told him it was actually Eden Park and Dunedin was a city on the South Island. Needless to say he copped it for that on the day, and a few times since. How he thought Eden Park was Dunedin Park I'll never know—particularly as there is even 'EDEN PARK' written across seats in one of the stands, which James Horwill has reminded Ant about a few times since.

The All Blacks were talking about the Rugby World Cup and the significance the Eden Park game had in the scheme of things, but we were not looking past the Bledisloe Cup and Tri-Nations—both of which were up for grabs. We had a forwards gathering before dinner the night before the match, and walked through our lineout options and talked about the importance of the contest. How we needed to match their intensity early on and then get on with it—and being relentless in our effort regardless of mistakes or decisions against us. There was a good vibe among the group and it was time to start thinking less about the game and instead get into a good head space.

As a distraction in the twenty-four hours leading up to the match, I had quite a bit of work to get through for EightyTwenty Vision and Heroes Boots. Luke was now working on it full time, but he would have to find another job if we couldn't find a way to supplement his income until Heroes could afford to employ him to run the business. It was taking a while to get another prototype of the boot—the first was was too expensive to be viable. It's proving hard to get things made ethically, yet still be able to compete with companies that produce their boots wherever they can as cheaply as they can.

I was still on Sydney time so I didn't go to sleep until around midnight the night before the match, and had a good sleep till 10AM the next morning. I then found a little cafe and was keen to finish off one of the books I was reading. Our first thing for the day was a meeting at 3PM when we went over the game plan again. There is an opportunity for the forwards to walk through lineouts or pass the ball around, or for the backs to walk through their starting plays. The group felt good and after talking briefly we went straight to our pre-game meal. I never feel like eating—the nerves by that time have you feeling a little bit nauseous and food is not so high on the list—but I got some food down and then headed to the physio room to stretch until strapping started at 4PM. It was a huge game and I was very excited about it.

Finally, it was our team meeting before leaving for the ground. Robbie didn't have much to say. It had been a two-week preparation and we had talked a lot about the game. 'There is one state that will cater for all our needs in this game. Body on fire, head in the fridge', was his message. He meant it was about getting out there and matching their intensity early, keeping cool heads and then pushing on with the game plan, holding on to the ball and denying them turnover ball and easy counter-attack, which we knew 80 per cent of their tries had come from.

Eden Park is a great venue and the field was good—firm, despite the rain that had been around, and a little slippery under foot—but it was a great night for rugby. The All Blacks started really well and we gave away a few penalties, which Dan Carter knocked over, and from there we never really got into the first half. We failed to hold onto the ball for a prolonged period of time to build pressure and played too wide rather than going through them, which they did very effectively to us.

The second half was somewhat different. We attacked well in parts and defended better, but a lapse at a kickoff gave them a really soft try immediately after we had given ourselves a slim chance with a try to Digby Ioane. The All Blacks capitalised on all their chances and it proved very hard to get back from the 17–0 deficit after half-time. We kept playing though, and managed to score another try to bring the score to 30–14 by the end. It was a very disappointing result and another step backwards after we had prepared so well.

The team was shattered. We had put so much preparation into the game and had failed to achieve what we planned. The All Blacks were good, but we knew we hadn't reached near our potential. We were soundly beaten on the scoreboard and we knew that we had let ourselves, and everyone back home, down.

# 12.
# Changing Tide
## Victory in Durban and Tri-Nations triumph in Brisbane

hen you lose, you cop it on the chin. The All Blacks were too good for us at Eden Park in early August of 2011. There was little time to mope though. We were straight into recovery in the change room: ten minutes on the stationary bike, followed by a stretch, and then ten minutes in the ice bin. The bus was due to leave for the airport at 3.30AM the next morning, when we started the long trip to our next match in South Africa, so there was no opportunity to sleep. After recovery and all our press commitments, and a few boys getting drugs-tested, we went back to the hotel to change into casuals and then on to an Italian restaurant to have a late dinner and hang out as a team. The dinner was a bit of a fizzer to start. Most of the team just sort of sat there staring into space, obviously contemplating the game that had just been and the missed opportunities. But after a while we managed to have a reasonable time, considering the circumstances, and after a few hours we were able to make a few jokes—many aimed at Ant Faingaa and his 'Dunedin Park' misunderstanding.

We were still in a fairly sombre mood, though, when we got back to the hotel to pack our bags. Then we boarded the bus and the long travel day had well and truly begun. Our flight path was Auckland to Sydney–Sydney to Johannesburg–Johannesburg to Durban—arriving late Sunday night. There is plenty that goes into getting a group of thirty-five people with lots of luggage around. Our management team do a great job sorting out all the logistics and ensuring (as much as possible) a smooth journey. Apart from our team manager, we have a full-time logistics and gear manager, Sam Cashman, who is a favourite among the boys. We know how hard he works and, although you never really see the work he does, he just makes everything run smoothly and has the right gear for when we need it and does a lot of work while we are travelling. Despite this, there are always the inevitable delays that are just part and parcel of group travel.

Personally, I was really looking forward to getting to Durban. My mum's sister Denise and her husband Barry live there with their three children: Jaymie, Tyler and Kim. We spent a lot of time on holiday with them growing up in Zimbabwe and I consider Tyler one of my closest friends. We always seem to pick up from where we left off, despite seeing each other once a year, at best, since we moved to Australia and they moved to Durban.

Twenty-seven hours later we arrived at the hotel in Durban. The team was pretty tired and most guys went straight to bed. I slept for half the flight from Sydney, then read for the remaining seven hours or so. It was such a luxury to have so much time to read and listen to music.

The first morning in Durban I was up at 5.30AM, bouncing off the walls. No one else, apart from a few members of the management staff, was awake. It's times like those that I really miss not having Richard Brown on tour. We often get out of the hotel early and do things—see the sights, take in some of the city—but it had to be a solo mission that morning. I cruised around until 9AM when I could get a local SIM card and contact my aunty and uncle, as all of my cousins were away when we first arrived.

Barry and Denise picked me up and took me to see a ship that had been washed up on the beach in the big storms. It was impressive to see, though potentially a tragedy for the environment if it didn't hold together until they could get it off the beach. Apparently, they would have to wait until the next spring tide to pull it off and take it to a salvage yard.

I had to be back at the hotel by 1PM for a press conference and a few interviews for the print media. In the afternoon, we had a flush cardio session on the bikes and then a pool session. Luke Burgess was splashing water everywhere and sneaking up behind guys and trying to wrestle. Eventually three of us wrestled him and well and truly had him under control. It was good to have a bit of a laugh after the disappointment of the game against the All Blacks. That night, I was asleep by 9PM. I was rooming with Lachie Turner for this trip, which was great. He is one of the politest young men you could meet and even cops it a fair bit from the guys for being so polite.

The next morning, it was time for an overall review of the game against New Zealand. We had a look at our defence and what we needed to work on, a review of our work at the breakdown and also a look at our restarts. From there, we came up with a list of focus points to work on, which were really helpful. It was a very thorough review and we came out of it with a clear understanding of where we fell short. We were too passive in defence, didn't slow their ball down enough and gave them too many opportunities to counter-attack from poor kicks and turnovers—and that's where the Kiwis excel. They have players with the ability to punish teams for these errors and convert them into points.

The team dinner that night was a good laugh after a fairly intense day. We split the group up according to 'rate your mop' (ie. your hair). There's the 'Too Thick' group led by James Horwill and Radike Samo, the 'Clutching/Bald' group with Rocky and Sharpie leading the charge, and I was in the 'Thinning Scissors/Just a Matter of Time' group with Will Genia. We both thought that was a bit harsh, but we were in good company with Matt Hodgson, Ben McCalman and Rob Simmons. Not a bad bunch of blokes to have dinner with. There was also the 'Gifted' group with the likes of Luke Burgess, James O'Connor and Ant Faingaa—guys who, at that point in time, had an immaculate head of hair with no fear of thinning.

The Springboks delayed announcing their team by a day, but we were fairly sure they would bring back all their big guns and it would be a vastly different team to the one that we had beaten in Australia a few weeks before. And so it proved a day later when they finally named what was a full-strength side, except for the absence of Schalk Burger.

There were a few heated training sessions at times that week. You could still sense the disappointment of the loss to the All Blacks and the underlying feeling that we needed to make up for it, so that led to a few disagreements and the odd scuffle. It was nothing too out-of-the-ordinary for training, but you could sense how big a game this was to everyone.

I was feeling a bit homesick the day before the match. I had only been away from Perth for five weeks, but I was probably also realising that I wouldn't be back there for at least another eleven or twelve weeks. It helped a bit to have breakfast with my cousin Tyler and his wife Nicolette, just around the corner from the hotel. We caught up on news and Tyler and I rehashed old stories of running amok on my grandfather's farm while growing up. I really value the few times I get to see Tyler when I travel to Durban with the Force and the Wallabies.

Saturday was game day and I was feeling really good. You could sense a buzz among the group—we were all really excited about the game. South Africa were back to their full strength team and it was going to be a real battle up front. Scrum and lineout would be crucial, but we had done a lot of work on those, so that gave us confidence. They would, no doubt, kick in behind us too—so we would have to work hard to get back and support, because they usually flood the breakdown if they get good pressure on the ball catcher.

It was an earlier game than usual—5PM kick-off. This was great as the late kick-offs make it a really long day of nerves and waiting and anticipation—you just want to get out there and play.

The intensity in the first twenty minutes was huge. Actually, the intensity in the entire first half was huge. They managed to get two penalties and threatened our line quite a few times. Tendai 'The Beast' Mtawarira made a few charging runs, but our scrambling defence managed to get back and defuse things. We had a few scrums on our five-metre line and we held up really well. It's an area that we had put a lot of work into during the week, so that was pleasing to see under that sort of pressure.

We threatened with quite a few line breaks but didn't manage to finish any. Right at the end of the first half we worked our way up to their line—only for referee Bryce Lawrence to blow his whistle and say it was our scrum and also half-time. We had the upper hand for the last five minutes of the first half, and to not get any points to show for it was disappointing. I was pretty annoyed. We had the ball and as I went to clear it the whistle had blown. I asked Bryce about the decision when we were running off the field for half-time, and he said that he had been knocked over and couldn't see what was going on so he had to reset play, which I guess is fair enough but just bad timing for us. Referees and players are obviously all doing their best, so it's great when referees can explain things like Bryce did.

Things were fairly calm in the dressing sheds at the break. It was important to use the ten minutes well and get a bit of a breather and talk about things that we needed to improve and things that we needed to keep doing. As forwards, we wanted to keep playing through them, to not get caught out too wide in attack, but rather attack closer and leave the space out wide for the backs. The ruck had improved from the week before and we wanted to keep putting the pressure on them in defence and targeting the breakdown for quick ball in attack. A lot of the guys in their team hadn't played for up to five weeks, so the second half was a good opportunity to maintain the intensity and see if they could maintain the energy levels they had brought to the first half.

We eventually managed to score a try through Pat McCabe in the corner after some great footwork by James O'Connor. James was kicking a lot better than the week before and kept the score ticking over. At one point we had a scrum and it was their ball around ten metres out from their line. The call came from our hooker, Stephen Moore, to have a crack at their scrum. We all knew what that meant—the aim was to go straight through their scrum and keep the push on. It worked and we got under them. Their scrum went backwards and spun around as their No. 8 Pierre Spies battled to clear it and the whistle blew—'scrum, gold ball'. The forward pack relished having the upper hand. We were all over them up front at that point and we were keen to keep the pressure on.

Stephen then said we were going to keep the ball in on our feed and go through them again. We knew their loose forwards would be keen to get off the scrum and defend against our backs, so we wanted to keep the ball in and scrummage eight against five, which drew the penalty and James kicked the three points to extend the lead. The game finished with them attacking hard on our line and eventually a tackle spilt the ball which Sekope Kepu flicked out to me and I kicked it up into the stands. There was a split second where 'Keps' looked at me with a somewhat bewildered look, before Bryce's whistle blew. I had been watching the stadium clock and we were a minute into overtime. We had won 14–9 and beaten the Springboks in South Africa to keep the goal of winning the Tri-Nations alive.

The boys were ecstatic. In the huddle on the field, Rocky talked about the importance of remembering the feeling—the intensity we had brought from the start and committing to preparing well in the future and giving ourselves every opportunity. Digby then got everyone to put their hands in the middle: 'Ok guys, LOVE on three. One, two, three … LOVE!', and we went off to the change room to our ice baths, media commitments and drugs testing, with the boom box blaring as we enjoyed the win. What a great feeling—a stark contrast to how we felt in Auckland one week before.

After training in the morning, we left Durban and travelled back to Sydney. It felt like we had been away for ages, even though it had only been two weeks, so I was looking forward to arriving in Sydney on the Wednesday.

I received a text message on that Wednesday night saying I was in the World Cup squad and it outlined the details for Thursday—an 8AM meeting, then a team photo and off to the Qantas maintenance hangar for the official team naming. Kurtley Beale and James O'Connor were late, but Kurtley turned up in time for the team photo. No one could get hold of James at all and he wasn't at the hotel, so we had the team photo and got ready for the big World Cup announcement without him. It was hugely frustrating to have someone, who you know wants to play well and wants the team to succeed, stuff up like this in a way that detracts from the team. It was a big distraction and added a lot of extra work for our media manager, Matt McIlraith, on what was already a huge day for him with the Rugby World Cup squad announcement. James's absence was also felt within the coaching and management team and probably higher up the ARU hierarchy too. So, while I supported him as a friend and teammate, we all knew that a one-game suspension, or something similar, was probably the inevitable outcome.

Robbie had told me that morning that Rocky was being replaced as captain by James Horwill. I was disappointed for Rocky, as I enjoyed his leadership and feel like he has won the trust and respect of the group and played a big part in ensuring our preparation was as thorough as possible, but could see how this might also allow him to focus on his own game more and allow him to rekindle that 'world's best' form that he was known for. Rocky's response when it was announced to the team in the morning, and the way he handled himself in the media, speaks volumes of the man that he is. He was very gracious about it and fully supportive of James as the new captain. Robbie said that Rocky's initial response was: 'If that's what is best for the team, then that's fine by me'.

The omission of Matt Giteau from the squad was somewhat overlooked given the change in captaincy and the whole thing with James. I was really disappointed for Matt, not just because he wouldn't be playing with the team anymore, but also for not having his presence at training and games or his legendary banter on and off the field. There is rarely a dull moment when he is around. When training and playing he gives his all and is the consummate professional—always doing extras and ensuring he is in the best possible condition physically, while also working on his game and trying to improve all the time.

I had emailed the squad a few weeks earlier about a possible question-and-answer session at an EightyTwenty fundraising dinner we were having in Brisbane on the Sunday after the All Blacks game. Out of the whole squad only Rocky and Nathan Sharpe replied, both saying that if I wanted them to be there, they would be. That means a lot when teammates are that genuine and supportive of your interests off the field.

Beyond all the hype of the Rugby World Cup squad announcement, the following week was a Test week. It was also one of the biggest matches many of us had played in up to that point: the All Blacks at a sold-out Suncorp Stadium in Brisbane to win the Tri-Nations. But the Monday and Tuesday headlines reflected anything but that. Instead, all the attention was on James O'Connor and the details surrounding him missing the team announcement. Then other stuff surfaced about an alleged altercation between Quade, James and Kurtley in Paris while we were on tour the year before. To the credit of the coaches and the squad, we got on with things and prepared on the Monday and Tuesday, although I wouldn't say it was the best training we have ever done—it was definitely an unwanted distraction.

The day off on Wednesday gave the squad a much-needed break from it all. I'd been feeling pretty tight so I booked a long massage in the morning, then had two radio interviews to promote the EightyTwenty dinner planned for the Sunday night. A wonderful woman, Ilenna, in Brisbane had volunteered her time to organise the dinner and had been liaising with Luke. We initially had a lot of people say they'd take a table, only to pull out with the RSVP date looming. It was amazing how much effort Ilenna put in, given that she works full-time and has a teenage son. It has been encouraging to find people who believe in the cause so much that they put so much of their time into it. We had a few people come through and book a table and one of our best supporters—a husband and wife who are involved for all the right reasons and don't want any public recognition for it—also organised three tables, while a few other tables were sold late to get the number up to twenty-one tables in total.

While there was a lot of stuff to do for the EightyTwenty dinner on the Sunday, my focus was on the Saturday game. I kept thinking about how big the opportunity was. It had been ten years since Australia held the Tri-Nations trophy, and after the Springboks had beaten the All Blacks at Port Elizabeth the week before we now had a chance to win it.

Thankfully, Thursday and Friday were good training days. The fiasco with James was behind us and it was announced that he was suspended for one match. Then the team was named. Radike Samo had made his way into the starting team and Adam Ashley-Cooper moved to the wing to bring Ant Faingaa into the centres. Ant had made an impact when he came on in Durban, and Radike would show just why he was picked at the back of the scrum, eventually scoring what was judged the 'try of the year' for the Wallabies.

On game day, I had a coffee with Luke and Bec O'Keefe, who had arrived for the fundraising dinner. I hadn't seen them for two months.

It was great to catch up a bit, hear how their boys were doing and how Kalen had begun spending hours just hanging out with the chickens in the backyard.

After coffee with the O'Keefes, I went home to say hello to Mum and Dad. A group of my dad's friends had been helping him build a counselling room extension at my parents place so my dad can work from home. He is doing his masters in counselling and loving the work. I went and had a look at what they were doing. From there it was back to the hotel for final preparations. I was pretty nervous, but mostly excited.

It had rained most of that day in Brisbane and we all expected a pretty wet game, which inevitably turns into a kicking fest with the forwards trying to win the war of attrition and the backs not getting too much of an opportunity. However, it stopped raining at around 6PM and kickoff was at 8PM. Suncorp Stadium has great drainage, so by the time kickoff came the field was in perfect condition with not too much moisture on it.

We started really well and made inroads into the All Blacks defensive line. Radike's try was great to watch. I had recovered a Genia box-kick and got up from the ruck to see the big man sprinting downfield in the clear. Two All Blacks were closing in on him, but the old man had the legs to get there and score an amazing try.

My back had started tightening up after a knock halfway through the first half, and by half-time it was pretty sore. The physios treated it through the break and when it was time for the second half I managed to get out there and hoped the adrenaline would kick in again and get me through the second half. The Kiwis starved us of the ball for the first twenty minutes of the second half and their forwards took control of the attack. They attacked narrow and made metres through the middle, eventually levelling the scores at 20–all after totally dominating possession for an extended period.

Will Genia provided the spark to get us back in the lead, when he went through a gap around the ruck and gave it to Digby who put Kurtley in the corner to make the score 25–20. We defended for much of the remaining period after that try and, with a few minutes to go, could sense that we were very close. It was right there, we just had to hold onto the ball. New Zealand forced the turnover and we were back in defence, but they finally gave away a penalty and Quade kicked the ball out to win the Tri-Nations trophy.

It was an amazing feeling. After the game, I was really keen to go out and enjoy the company of the guys, but my back was pretty sore. Standing up was too uncomfortable and sitting down was even worse, so I ended up going straight to bed once we were back at the hotel, lying there talking to Emma until we both fell asleep.

Sunday was the day of the EightyTwenty dinner. I had a medical at 7AM after a few hours sleep. There was quite a bit of media coverage around Quade being sighted for an alleged knee to Richie McCaw's head. He was eventually let off by the SANZAR judicial officer but was copping quite a bit of heat about it from the New Zealand media. At the time, I remember thinking that it would be interesting to see if it would still be something people were talking about once we arrived in New Zealand for the tournament. Sure enough it was, and that event (off the back of a series of squabbles with McCaw since our match in Hong Kong the year before) resulted in Quade being labelled 'public enemy No. 1' upon our arrival in New Zealand for the Rugby World Cup.

It was tough to pick myself up for the EightyTwenty dinner, as I was pretty sore and just generally pretty drained from the game and the build-up to it all. Luke and Bec picked us up from the hotel in the morning. We had a meeting at 10.30AM at BlackStar in West End—it's a comfort knowing BlackStar coffee is totally ethical.

I was feeling somewhat uncomfortable about the dinner. It was at a pretty fancy place on the Brisbane River and we would, hopefully,

ABOVE: Brownie and I after the win against the Barbarians at Wembley in 2008.

BELOW: Luke O'Keefe and I fixing the car on one of our trips to Zimbabwe.

ABOVE: Clowning about with Nick Cummins on Lake Wakatipu in Queenstown when we played the Highlanders.

BELOW: Quade Cooper, James O'Connor, Brad Hilyard, myself and Richard Colreavy at my 21st birthday party in 2009.

ABOVE: White water rafting on the mighty Zambezi in 2008—Luke O'Keefe and I at the front of the raft.

BELOW: Talking with a group of conservation farming workers on a recent trip to Nkayi, Zimbabwe.

LEFT: Me, Ronald, Paul and Luke at the opening of a granary for orphans and vulnerable people in the Nkayi community.

BELOW: Emma and I enjoying an African sunset.

ABOVE: Jarrod McKenna shares a homily at our wedding.

BELOW: Michael and I sitting at the table he and I made from discarded decking materials.

ABOVE LEFT: Quade, Will and I after retaining the Nelson Mandela trophy with our win against South Africa in Sydney in 2011.

ABOVE RIGHT: Sharing a laugh with James O'Connor after the Tri-Nations win in Brisbane in 2011.

LEFT: Dinner down at the beach with Em while I was out injured during the Force season in 2011.

ABOVE: Kurtley, Salesi, Ben and I after winning the Tri-Nations, Brisbane, 2011.

BELOW: On the way to my first try against Russia in Nelson during Rugby World Cup 2011.

LEFT: With my brothers Steve and Mike at a fundraising dinner for EightyTwenty after the Bledisloe Cup test in Brisbane in 2011.

LEFT: In the defensive line with Ben McCalman and Berrick Barnes in the bronze medal play-off against Wales.

raise a lot of money to be used to help people in Nkayi. But it all seemed a bit wrong that we could raise money, while eating the best food and drinking the best wine, when the people we were helping had so little. The divide is great. But I'm so grateful for the support EightyTwenty receives as it's this support that allows us to continue to help close that divide. Our work in Nkayi had been guided by a desire to help people in poverty, not take control of their lives. My understanding of the way Jesus lived was that he wanted people to take control of their own lives, to remove selfish ambition and to 'love our neighbour as we would ourselves'.

I was shattered on the Sunday. It had been a huge game, and incredibly draining, but I had to lift myself up for the dinner. It all went reasonably well. Nick Farr-Jones was good enough to offer his services as MC. I gave a speech about the work we were doing in Nkayi and the areas we were involved with. Em, Luke and I had talked about trying to speak in a way that presented our project in terms of the people in Nkayi, and how they were taking initiative rather than presenting them as victims (as so much development and charity fundraising tends to do). We were conscious of not trying to emotionally manipulate the people at the dinner into giving money. In my speech I gave an overview of the work we were doing, as well as some personal stories of people I had met whose lives had been bettered. We also showed a video that showed what was happening on the ground and introduced the team in Nkayi.

Afterwards, someone came up to me to say my speech was not very good and that I should have tried to 'milk' the room and that I needed to take public speaking classes. I was stunned. I understood what he was saying, but I wasn't prepared to sell myself to a crowd for donations. I know some people only turn up to EightyTwenty events because of my rugby profile, and while that may mean we raise extra money, it isn't a sustainable income stream for the work we want to achieve. I also feel that it undervalues the hugely important work that Luke does as well.

Despite the dinner's success, I went home feeling lousy. Luke and I both felt burdened by finding the balance between raising money to fund the projects we want to do, but in a way that we felt comfortable with, ethically and sustainably. For example, selling shoes made in sweatshops to fund a charity might seem justifiable but, in reality, you are not addressing the root of the problem—the exploitation of people who are then 'helped' with the excess profits of their very exploitation.

Despite part of me just wanting a bit of a break away from rugby after the Tri-Nations triumph and the success of our fundraising effort in Brisbane, I could feel the excitement of being part of my first Rugby World Cup growing—being part of an Australian team that was committed to each other and to representing the country as best as we could. We had improved a lot as a group and had done something that hadn't been done for a long time—win the Tri-Nations. But there were now much bigger fish to fry. As Robbie has put it a few times over the last couple of years, 'The world is your oyster'. It was now time to realise our ultimate goal on rugby's greatest stage in New Zealand.

# 13.

## Game On
### A memorable Maori welcoming before victory over Italy

There was little time to savour the Tri-Nations victory as we only had one week to go before leaving for the Rugby World Cup in New Zealand. It was a short series, but still quite draining because of the fast turnaround between games among all of the travel. I was in a lot of pain for a few days after the victory over the All Blacks, and our first team training session, back in Sydney on the Tuesday afternoon, had a few walking wounded. It had been a really intense match. Playing the entire second half after my back had started stiffening up no doubt aggravated the muscles a fair bit. I had got through a lot of work in the game and it was very physical at the breakdown. I was just taking longer than usual to recover.

After training on the Tuesday afternoon the whole squad had a signing session for almost two hours, signing Rugby World Cup jerseys, team photos, and so on. It becomes quite tedious signing your name four hundred times and my signature does seem to deteriorate after a while, but these signing sessions are all part of it and there is generally little complaining. A few of the boys had a chuckle when we saw Robbie signing the 'team photo' of the Rugby World Cup squad, which had James O'Connor photo-shopped into the back row.

I was in bed just after 8PM on Tuesday evening when my phone rang. It was Robbie. He said he wanted me to get away from the hotel

179

and have the day off on Wednesday. I was still tired and sore and the medical staff wanted me to have a break too. I usually feel guilty missing sessions when the rest of the boys are training, but it was a big relief this time. I headed down to the gym at 8AM to help out with a video that our dietician was putting together for junior rugby players, then did some weights around my shoulder, before heading back to the hotel for another sleep. I woke up at 11.30AM feeling a lot better, and then got out of the hotel with Em and caught a bus to Balmain for a look around. It's a really nice part of Sydney and I felt far enough away from the hotel to be the break that Robbie and the medical staff asked of me.

I was back into training on the Thursday with a skills session and weights in the morning, then we all had the afternoon off for the John Eales Medal dinner that evening. Partners and families came into the hotel for the afternoon and it was great to see Radike Samo's kids running around the foyer.

The John Eales Medal has a lot of significance in Australian rugby. It's named after the living legend of Australian rugby who played eighty-six Tests, fifty-five of them as captain. John Eales remains the most successful captain the Wallabies have ever had. He won two Rugby World Cups (1991 and 1999) and led a golden era for Australian rugby that commenced with a thrill-nil whitewash of the All Blacks to claim the Bledisloe Cup in 1998 and ended with a Tri-Nations/Bledisloe Cup double in 2001 after also defeating the British and Irish Lions that same year. His list of achievements is long and, personally, it was a great thrill to receive the medal in 2010 from the man himself.

What also makes this award so special is that it is voted for by the players after each game. I felt really honoured and fortunate to win it in 2010, but I knew that I was not in with a real chance. I thought it would come down to Kurtley Beale or Will Genia, with Stephen Moore being an outside chance, given his 2011 form.

It was a fun evening seeing some highlights from the games over the preceding year. Before the announcement of the medal winner, they had a sort of elimination thing, which was quite humorous with five cameras sending live feeds of the top five players left in the count up onto the big screen. As it counted down to the winner, they announced who had polled fifth, fourth, third, second, in a game show-style elimination process, with the various contenders dropping off the big screen as they were eliminated. I had come third and Em had a lot of fun with the process, eventually nudging me with that elimination-type sound 'bap bow' as my video feed disappeared from the big screen. She is never one to miss an opportunity to have fun, often at my expense, and this was one such occasion.

After I was eliminated it came down to Kurtley and Stephen Moore, who were both very deserving in their own right. Kurtley won it and I was so happy for him. He was rookie of the year in 2010 and had continued to improve throughout 2011 and showcase just what he can do on the field. What he has acheived is even more impressive when you hear the obstacles he has overcome in his life, as an Aboriginal kid growing up in Sydney's west. His mum and his aunty were there that night and you could tell it meant a lot to him. You could also see how proud his mother was—she couldn't hold back the tears as Kurtley went up to accept his medal from John Eales.

That night was the last of the major formalities in Australia ahead of the World Cup. There was a certain air of excitement around it, with all of us hoping that the best highlights of our year were still to come in New Zealand. We trained on the Friday morning after the dinner and it was a really sharp session, with everyone putting in a lot of effort knowing that we had a relatively free weekend before leaving on the Monday.

On the Friday afternoon, the forwards were doing weights and one of the props was leg pressing sets of five with around 500 kilograms of weight. He claimed to have an upset stomach and during his last set, after fatigue had no doubt set in, he pushed a bit more out than he intended too from his rear end. He quickly finished the last two reps and got off the machine to grab some sanitising agent that was around the gym to wipe down the stuff that was left on the leg press machine. He was a bit embarrassed about it, but fairly tired too and the forwards seemed happy enough to let it slide. He was training hard and that's what we do, we train hard and leave most of the talking to the backs.

That is where the event turned bad for this poor prop. The forwards were done and the backs were on their way in to do their weights. Drew Mitchell had arrived and caught the end of the commotion with the front rower cleaning his watery poo off the leg press machine and that was it. Drew then stood at the top of the stairs re-telling the story, with much gusto, to everyone as they arrived at weights. He was so tickled by the story that he even thought it tweet-worthy … 'One of our props shed blood, shit and tears in the gym today … I won't say who but he was very embarrassed #littlepoopoo #weebum'. It's fair to say that poor prop hasn't lived it down since, with the nickname 'Poo poo' getting a fair bit of airtime.

After weights and a cycle session at the gym on Saturday morning I was off for the weekend. It felt good to get some balance before the World Cup. Matt, Naomi and Amelie Noffs picked us up for breakfast, and we walked around two of Sydney's parks and talked and hung out for the morning. I tried to keep it casual as much as possible, though Matt and I still used the chance to discuss a few things around Heroes Boots and how things were progressing. Our ethical boot was throwing up quite a challenge, but we were still up for it.

Em and I went out for Mexican in the evening and then went to the movies to see *The Help*—a film, based on a novel, that tells the story of three black maids working in white households in the southern states of America in the early 1960s. It was very sad in parts but it also showed the resilience of the black women and their brilliant sense of humour despite the segregation and racism they encountered daily. I was really moved by the film, perhaps a little more than most because I had witnessed similar circumstances during my time growing up in Zimbabwe.

We were farewelled in Australia with a fairly modest ceremony at Sydney Town Hall around lunchtime on Monday 3 September. We were all pretty keen to just get over to New Zealand by that stage, but it was nice to see some diehard fans and a few business suits with gold scarves out to send us on our way.

We had already sent some bags over by freight, but still had to pack up and be ready for a 3.45AM 'bags on bus' and 4AM departure from the hotel on the Tuesday. This was finally it. We were off to the Rugby World Cup.

Dressed in our suits and milling around the hotel foyer at 4AM, a few boys still looked pretty sleepy. 'Bed head' was definitely the hairstyle most were sporting, with the exception of James O'Connor and the 'gifted mops'—whose hair is always impeccable.

We were fortunate enough to fly to New Zealand in business class, which was a nice change compared with my last flight to Auckland with Ben McCalman and our forwards coach Patricio Noriega sharing my row. To be able to lie down and sleep was a real treat and I did for the entire flight—from take-off, right through to when we had to put our chair upright for landing.

On our arrival at Auckland airport, there was a brief welcoming ceremony for us with a welcome, which included some Maori singing and a prayer. We then headed to the hotel. It was all go from there and after checking in we had half an hour before getting on the bus again, this time to head to training. It was an open session and there were around a thousand Tongans all dressed in red when we arrived, which seemed odd, but we soon found out that the Tongan team were training after us. Given that seven thousand Tongans were at the airport to greet their team a couple of days before, it wasn't surprising that they had a strong contingent ready to watch them train. There were a few Aussie supporters around, but certainly not at the Tongan level.

Given we were playing Italy in our first match on the Sunday, we did our normal Monday session at training despite it being Tuesday. It was a fairly quick session and then we were back to the hotel with only half an hour to be in our number ones (our smart clothes) and on the bus again to our official welcoming ceremony in Auckland.

The ceremony was amazing. It was a traditional Maori welcoming called a *pōwhiri*. It started with the *wero* (challenge) as we approached a group of men and women, and the men began to cautiously advance towards us with ceremonial weapons, calling out battle cries and generally looking pretty mean. As we approached them, the *karanga* (call out or summons) took place with two of the women singing to each other. The *wero* intensified as we approached each other. Then our captain, James Horwill, leaned forward and picked up the *rautapu* (a symbolic offering of a carved effigy with leaves tied to it). Then they escorted us to our seats on the stage where the speeches took place before we were given our Rugby World Cup caps and we each performed a *hongi* (a greeting where you press your noses together) with the most senior Maori man present. We were officially welcomed and, after a quick photo opportunity for the press, we signed autographs for people who had come to watch it all unfold. It was quite a memorable welcome and something I'll be sure to look back on fondly for many years to come.

I was in bed by 9PM on our first night in New Zealand. It had been a long day after the early start and it felt so good to get into bed that first night. I felt really refreshed the next morning and made my way down to the gym with Dan Vickerman for a quick session. We had nothing on until a team meeting at 10.30AM, but Vicks and I both wanted to get a bit of work done. He's another teammate with a great story surrounding his path to the Rugby World Cup, having gone off to Cambridge University for three years from 2008 to do his studies, before deciding he wasn't quite done with rugby and giving it another crack. He had very limited chances to show Robbie and the selectors he was up to it, but sure enough he grabbed those chances and made the most of them. He's a really impressive guy.

Training was fairly heated on the Wednesday with some full contact breakdown work and then an opposed training run where we run 'opposition strategy'. All the reserves and 'double dirties' run as a team, then we run with our strategy against them and they defend. The term 'double dirties' describes those eight players in the squad who are outside the match-day twenty-two but still part of the thirty-man squad. The session can get pretty intense. Robbie usually says, 'Shoulders on, no legs', meaning get in front and stop a bloke's progress, but no belting each other. Some guys find it hard to restrain themselves and it usually only takes a few phases or one good clean out, and the boys are into it. If you don't slow down the attacking team's ball it becomes an unrealistically fast ball and it is a lot harder to defend. This training gives us good preparation going into the game and the opposition always keep you honest at training. In the huddle at the end of these training sessions that have elements of full contact, we have a few 'slow dances'— guys nominated by the team to slow dance with each other in the circle, to ensure they leave behind any tension they may have built up on the training field. It's pretty funny and the guys usually have a good laugh.

Our cameraman, Kong (his name is Anthony or 'AJ' but everyone calls him Kong; I don't even know why—in fact I reckon a few boys don't even know his real name), asked us to start a new segment he wanted to film called 'photo club', where we all put our photos together every week and pick the three best and then share them with the public through a video that Kong puts together and posts on the Wallabies website. I collect the forwards, Adam Ashley-Cooper the backs, and

Sam Cashman collects the photos from the management team and then we film the segment. It adds a bit of 'colour', as Kong likes to say, so we filmed that on the Wednesday evening after training. I guess we were fairly reluctant participants and Adam Ashley-Cooper stitched me up and said that I had come up with the idea, but that's to be expected from Coops—he never misses an opportunity have a laugh. Kong has been with the Wallabies longer than anyone else currently in our squad. He follows us everywhere, filming all our press conferences and training and putting footage together for the website and TV stations in Australia, when we are away on tour. He is very good at what he does and the team loves having him around.

Thursday was our day off ahead of the Italy game and it came at a good time after some fairly intense training the day before. I was up at 5AM and couldn't sleep, so I spent some time reading. I was reading a novel, which is not usually my go, called *Jasper Jones* by Craig Silvey and I really enjoyed it.

Then I went to review some more footage of the Italian team. I tend to do a lot of analysis of opposing teams as it gives you a good idea of what to expect in games. We don't get to play Italy all that much, so watching some of their more recent games was our best way of working out where their strengths lie and what could be possible target areas.

My first World Cup press conference was a bit of fun. There were a lot of foreign journos around, so it was a good chance to see the different styles in journalism and what they wanted to talk about. Few Aussie journos want to dissect the scrum performance, but many of the Italian and northern hemisphere journos are well up for it.

I had an interview with a French journo who had caught out James Horwill the day we arrived by asking if he could name three Italian players—he couldn't. The journo asked me the same thing and luckily I had been looking at a lot of footage and rattled off a few of their players' names. They're a decent team. Their scrum is big and strong. They like to dominate opposition scrums—and they often do—so that was a big challenge for us and it was talked about quite a bit at the press conference.

After the conference, we had to do interviews with some of the Australian print media who had a disagreement with the IRB regarding accreditation and had boycotted the process. We were having to accommodate them on the side, separate to the main press conferences, but it was a necessity because the agencies that boycotted the accreditation process happened to control all the main newspapers in Australia. I didn't know the full extent of it, but I did know that it was in the game's interest in Australia for this section of the media to be reporting on the Wallabies and the Rugby World Cup, so we were happy to help.

Some quick physio treatment after the press conference and then I enjoyed the afternoon off with Em, who had bussed in from Auckland's North Shore to meet me for a walk around. Em was staying with friends of my parents who were originally from Zimbabwe. We found a good bunch of op shops and I managed to find a few pairs of shorts for summer. It's hard to find shorts that fit well in Australian op shops I find—maybe they get bought quickly? Or no one throws out half-decent summer shorts?

It was great to hang out with Em and get away from the hotel. I find that if I don't get out I get lethargic and just generally in a bad mental state. I have come to the conclusion that people are definitely not made for hotel living. Well, I'm certainly not cut out for it anyway.

On the Thursday evening before our first match, a group of fifteen or so players and staff went across the road to a Pacific Islands convention to meet Prime Minister Julia Gillard before she travelled back to Australia. Her partner, Tim, was down at training and seemed like a really good bloke—he loved passing the ball around and talking to the boys.

I had not met Julia Gillard before and was looking forward to hopefully being able to have a bit of a chat. There was a lot of media and it was somewhat awkward for a while as the publicity part of it took place, but the media were eventually cleared from the room and we were able to have a chat to the PM. I have quite an interest in politics and was keen to see what she was like in person. I found her really engaging, very articulate and interesting. She was telling us how Ban Ki Moon had just returned from a visit to Kiribati and he had been talking at the United Nations summit about what the real impact that climate change and rising sea levels was having for that nation.

I asked her about a few things and raised my concerns over some issues. She was gracious and we chatted about various different problems. I didn't think she was going to take much on board from some rugby player, but figured I probably wouldn't get many opportunities like that one. I copped a bit of grief from the boys on the way back to the hotel, with a few saying I 'hogged conversation with her and they couldn't get a word in' or that I was the PM's aide. It was good banter.

There was no dinner at the hotel by the time we made it back, so a group of us headed for sushi across the road. The waiter's face lit up when he saw a big group of us heading in—they were going to make some decent money off our lot. Cliffy Palu, Digby, James O'Connor, Kurtley, Quade, Salesi, James Horwill, Luke Burgess, Berrick Barnes and myself all in one sitting—there was a lot of sushi eaten.

Kurtley had lost a game of 'scissor, paper, rock' to James and Quade and had to buy them both dinner. I didn't realise this at the time and nearly mentioned to Quade that I'd never seen him eat so much sashimi. Kurtley wasn't impressed when the bill was close to NZ$200 for the three of them, but he begrudgingly paid it after a lot of banter and allegations of rigging. They're clearly good mates and it's fairly common to hear the screams and carry-on when they are playing video games at the hotel. Everybody knows who wins.

The captain's run was brought forward to Friday due to North Harbour Stadium hosting another game on Saturday night and we continued with our usual Test week preparation, which meant it was technically our Thursday session. We trained well and tried to focus on the breakdown without doing too much contact as we had done a lot on the Wednesday. Training is different when a lot of media are around. They get to stay for the first fifteen minutes, so during that time we do more fun, warm-up type stuff, not working on anything in particular. They must think we are a bunch of jokers who don't take training very seriously, but we knuckle down and do some hard work once they leave.

Back at the hotel, after the captain's run we had a press conference. Will Genia, James Horwill, Robbie and myself were put forward. The Italian coach Nick Mallet had come out and said they were focusing on their game against Ireland, knowing they would probably not beat us, but we all knew he was just stirring the pot. There were quite a few questions about looking ahead to the Irish game, but the team had talked about it as players and there was no way we were going to take the Italians lightly. We struggled the previous two times we'd played them in Italy, and they were a team that had improved a lot under Nick Mallett's coaching and had even beaten France in the 2011 Six Nations.

I did some weights before seeing the physios for some treatment and a massage. Then we went for a team dinner before coming back to the hotel to watch the opening game—New Zealand v Tonga. Dinner was great. I sat with Quade and Radike. Radike told me about how he got to Australia. After leaving Fiji, he moved to Canberra to play club rugby, and then made his way into the Brumbies team. He was overlooked by Fiji for the 2003 Rugby World Cup, only to debut for Australia in 2004. It was an amazing story in itself and when you consider it alongside his latest renaissance it was even more impressive.

As we were walking back to the hotel after dinner, the final fireworks display to open the Rugby World Cup began. It was huge, with fireworks all over the city. I saw a few birds scurrying from tree to tree—they looked petrified.

The opening game went pretty much as expected with the All Blacks dominating from early on, but Tonga put in a really decent second half. The New Zealand public seem like a fairly tough crowd to please, and it was interesting to see how the commentators immediately jumped on how the All Blacks looked a bit scratchy in the second period. Maybe they did take their foot off it a bit after having a fairly comfortable lead, but there was certainly no reason to be too concerned. It was still an easy victory to the home side.

In keeping with our usual match routine, we did a second captain's run at a different ground on the Saturday morning and then we had the afternoon off. Em came into the city again from the North Shore and we spent the afternoon together. We walked around and found a park where we hung out for a while. It was great to get away from the hotel again.

Sunday was game day. Our first match for Rugby World Cup 2011 and I was really excited. I woke up and opened the curtain—it was pouring down. Rain was forecast but you never know with weather forecasts in Auckland—it seems to change a lot and redefines the saying 'four seasons in one day'.

It was still bucketing down later on and it was clearly going to be a wet-weather game. It was an earlier kick-off time, so there was less sitting around and waiting for the game, which was great. We were strapped up and ready to go for a 1.40PM team meeting before we left for the ground. Robbie didn't say much, but just reminded us that the talk was over and it was now time to play, 'This is for real. It'll be like nothing we've experienced this year, and if you've watched any of the other games you would have realised that they will be desperate.'

I got quite emotional during the national anthem—I was thinking of how much hard work had gone into getting to where I was, how much help I've had along the way, and how many times I had dreamt of this moment growing up. I was at a Rugby World Cup. The talk was over—it was time to play.

Italy were tough opponents and they gave us nothing. We had to work for all our points. The first half was hard going, they disrupted our ball and there were a lot of penalties. At half-time Robbie talked about staying composed and sticking to our guns—the holes would open up if we held onto the ball long enough. Sure enough they did and we scored some good tries in the second half to secure the four-try bonus point, which was great. I was subbed at sixty minutes for Ben McCalman who did really well when he came on, as did the other reserves, particularly James O'Connor who scored a try and kicked well. He was clearly on a mission to regain his starting place after being suspended for his mishap around the squad announcement. In the end, we had a fairly comfortable victory after a close first half. It was a good hit-out for our first match of the tournament.

After the game, a few boys were drug tested and there was a walk-through media session. This is when a whole heap of journos can talk to you if they want to, but if they don't then you head back to the change room. Dan Vickerman won our 'Man of Gold' player-of-the-match award. He is a tireless worker and puts everything into the game. You can't help but be inspired by his fiery determination.

Since the match was played a bit earlier, it gave us a chance to go to the pool for a team recovery session. We had a bit of a relay and then stretched. We were fairly content with the result, which came off the back of a dominant second-half performance. But everyone knew there was a lot of improvement left in us and there was only a six-day turnaround before our next game against Ireland—our biggest match of the pool stage. It would prove to be an eventful week and my personal frustrations were tested more than ever because my back injury flared up unexpectedly. My Rugby World Cup dream was under threat once again.

# 14.

## Injury Frustrations
### Shock loss to Ireland before the USA fronts up

Monday morning after the victory over Italy and we were straight into it again. We had medicals and physio in the morning, icing the aches from the night before, and we went over the footage of the game, looking at our strategy in detail. We identified areas that worked for us and things we needed to improve on. We gave too many penalties away and let them control field position in the first half by not building sustained pressure. That had to be improved on before we came up against an opponent like Ireland.

In the afternoon we had another recovery session at a pool, with more swimming and stretching and a fair bit of skylarking from the boys. Adam Ashley-Cooper did a back flip off the ten-metre diving board, which was amazing to see. I know a lot of people do it with ease, but it's not your everyday rugby player's go-to trick. Apparently, during a camp before the last World Cup, the team had a day off at a crowded beach in Portugal and Adam climbed up a cliff on one side of the beach before performing a perfect back flip to a standing ovation from beach goers. Coops is quite a character and a bit of a thrillseeker as well it seems.

It was a short week until our next match, so two days after the Sunday match we were into our team review and preview ahead of the Ireland game. They were a different proposition altogether, with threats all over the field. They have a solid forward pack, with a very strong and mobile back row and a good backline that includes the likes of Brian O'Driscoll—a proven gamebreaker who can punish teams if given too much room and he can also create opportunities when not given much room at all.

The afternoon was our normal flush session with passing races and sideline defence games, which were quite heated. Everyone seemed a bit on edge. We knew that we were going to have to improve our performance to beat Ireland. It was continuous rugby with no break after the game against Italy. You are living with each other in hotels and no doubt everyone was looking forward to the following day to get away from it and get some balance.

On the Wednesday, I had breakfast with the friends from Zimbabwe who Em was staying with, and then wandered down to the Rugby World Cup 'Fanzone'. We encountered a massive crowd of Samoan supporters who literally took over the bus station—rushing the street every time a car with Samoan flags drove past, chanting, 'Manu, Manu, Manu!' It was amazing to watch.

It is remarkable the way sport can bring people together and how it can be used for good. Take the way Nelson Mandela tried to unify South Africa in 1995 around the Rugby World Cup, trying to reclaim what was once a symbol of apartheid South Africa—the Springboks—and turn them into something that could bring black and white South Africans together. Although there was, and possibly still are, parts of the black South African community who don't support the Springboks, you have to say that Mandela did an amazing job of using the World Cup for that purpose.

From my own experience, I'm forever grateful for the friends I have made through sport, the disciplines and self control I have learnt and the opportunities it has given me. Perhaps the most significant is the chance to work with EightyTwenty Vision in Zimbabwe and see how sport can bring so much happiness to those communities. One of the smaller things that we have done on the ground in Nkayi is organise an annual soccer and netball competition among the schools. To see the gusto with which those girls and boys play soccer and netball is something to behold. The delight and sense of achievement and community they get, from something as simple as a day of sports, has been amazing.

We resumed full preparation for the next game on the Thursday and I made it through training pretty well, but in the afternoon my back started tightening up quite a bit. The big knock I received against New Zealand in the first half of the Tri-Nations decider back in Brisbane had been niggling me leading into the tournament. I managed to get through the Italian game, but it tightened right up and by the Friday was giving me a lot of pain. I had physio on the Friday morning and then went off and had a scan instead of going to the captain's run, because the medical team were worried there was damage to a disc.

On the Friday afternoon I had seven different physiotherapy appointments. One of the physios stayed behind at the hotel and I met him pretty much on the hour for twenty to thirty minutes each time. That released it a little bit, but it was still pretty irritable. There was nothing more we could do and I just needed to get a good sleep and see how it pulled up Saturday morning. I eventually managed to get some rest but the discomfort of my back was overshadowed by worried thoughts about not being all right the following morning. I desperately wanted to play against Ireland with my teammates. Finally, a bit of deep breathing and contemplative prayer/meditation did the trick and I was out for the night.

The coaches had given me until the morning to prove my fitness, but getting up on that Saturday it was pretty clear that I'd be more of a hindrance than a help. The call was made to pull me from the team. Ben McCalman would start at openside flanker in my place and Wycliff Palu came onto the bench.

Robbie had a good chat with me and said I needed to really pull back on the training I was doing and trust in the conditioning I had done. He urged me to make my only focus getting back to playing. Then, after the World Cup, we would talk about how I had been training and how to be smarter about it in the future. I was very grateful that Robbie took the time to talk to me on game day, as I felt really bad pulling out. I had never done that before and know the potential disruption it has on the group. I was really disappointed with myself and felt like I was letting my teammates down, which I was. But in this instance I had no control over it. The doc took me to a hospital at lunchtime on the Saturday to have an epidural to try and speed up the recovery process and get me back as soon as possible.

It was one of those situations when you know that you would let them down even more if you did start and then came off in the first few minutes. Mum and Dad had flown in on the Friday night, so that was poor timing, but they were still really happy to see me and I managed to catch up with them and have a coffee and a bit of lunch.

In the afternoon I went and saw a back specialist and received some advice. Thankfully the scans showed up no disc damage, so we were looking at one to two weeks recovery. I was instructed to lay low and stay in bed for a few days, which was always going to be challenging. I really don't like lazing around too much. I decided to go and buy a few Sean Penn films to help me take it easy. He's an actor I really enjoy watching—I even like a few of the films he's produced and directed. I stocked up on a few of those and between that and looking at footage of teams we might play later in the competition, I had enough to keep me busy during my period of laying low.

It was tough to watch the match that night against Ireland at Eden Park. Our biggest game of the pool stage and there I was lying in my hotel room nursing a back injury. I had been told to stay in bed for the game, but it was hard for me to keep still. The match didn't go as well as any of us hoped and it was difficult to watch. Ireland were smart in the way they attacked the breakdown and played field position. They never really looked like scoring, apart from the intercept late in the match, but they definitely deserved the win because of the way they built pressure and scored points.

Ireland threw a lot of numbers into the breakdown and their scrum drew a lot of penalties. It's really hard, as a team, to build pressure when your set pieces are under pressure and the guys were struggling in both the scrum and lineout. It was so disappointing and that loss would make it a lot more difficult in the quarter-finals and semi-finals. I tried not to look too far ahead, but it was hard not to see from all the coverage that our likely path from that point was going to be a quarter-final against the Springboks and a semi-final against the All Blacks.

You do have to beat just about every team to win the tournament so if we were going to do it we were going to do it the hard way now. We had made it a lot tougher for ourselves, but we had to live with that and improve. I tried to stay up after the match and wait for all the boys to come back to hang out for a bit, but I really just needed to lie down and get off my back and rest up so I called it a night.

When I woke on the Sunday I still had that empty feeling. We never managed to turn our pressure into points and battled around the set piece. Ireland stymied our attack by holding us up and not letting us get quick ball. Not getting that front foot ball—so important to our game plan—really crippled us. We also lacked field position at key times and allowed them to get back into the game through our mistakes.

Personally it was hugely disappointing. It was the first time I have ever had to pull out of a game after being named in the team. I'd mentally prepared really well before the game and had looked at a lot of their footage. I really enjoy playing Ireland and the match was one that I had looked forward to from the moment I first saw our World Cup draw. There was no way I was going to get through the game, but

I so wished I could have played.

We travelled to Wellington on the Sunday afternoon following the loss to Ireland. It was nice to get out of Auckland and I really enjoy Wellington. It has a much different vibe to it. It seems a bit more chilled out and it's not as big. Before leaving Auckland I managed to have breakfast with Emma, Mum and Dad. They had picked up a campervan and were going to make their way to Wellington to watch the USA game before Dad had to fly back to uni and work. I was really hoping to be able to play against the Americans, so they could at least see me in one Rugby World Cup game. But it wasn't to be.

I was doing rehab on my back four times a day in the early part of the week leading up to the USA game. There were a lot of exercises I had to do, so that took up a bit of my time, but I was also forced to lay low a bit more and lie in bed and lounge around, which I really hate. However, it did give me a lot of time to read and reflect. It felt like a very long time since I was back in Perth and I felt a bit homesick again. I missed my friends, Luke and Bec O'Keefe and their boys, and Richard Brown too. Being away for so long is just part of playing professional rugby and I definitely do feel the distance of my friends.

I was able to spend a lot more time with Emma while I was injured, which was really great. I definitely consider her my best friend and it was so good for me to be able to get away from the team environment and spend time with her and laugh and joke about things and have a bit of time away. I'm not the most extroverted person, so I guess I need to find a bit of space for myself away from the boys so that when I am with the team I can add more value and be a part of things. I started getting on really well with Luke Burgess while injured and we had some good chats. I passed on *Jasper Jones*, which I read in a couple of days, and he enjoyed it too.

In the days that I had been thinking about how much I missed home, I received a nice text message from our housemate Ailsa to see how I was going. She's hilarious—she knows almost nothing about rugby, but is such an excitable person and when we win I get these wild, enthusiastic text messages, sometimes a few days after we play, saying that she just found out that we had won and how great it was and she's sure I played well. True to form she had done a web search to see what the Wallabies were doing and she sent a text to say that she saw that I missed the game and hoped I was doing okay.

I moved in with Ailsa in February 2010 after my brother Steve and another bloke moved out. I was left with a big house and a big rent and managed to break the lease. Through a friend I heard Ailsa needed someone to move in to her place for a few months. When I bought a place in Perth in May 2010 Ailsa moved in. So Alisa, Em and me live together and it works out really well. We love her to bits. I was looking forward to seeing her, whenever that might be.

We had a long team meeting after lunch on the Tuesday following the loss to Ireland and talked about the ways that we needed to improve or go back to things that have worked for us in the past. We nutted out a few of our shapes and got everyone on the same page. This took a good hour and a bit, but by the end of the session you could sense that we knew where we had to get to in terms of on-field play. We all came away realising that World Cup rugby is different to other rugby we play—it's more defence oriented and you rarely get away with trying to attack from your own end. The referees were also giving away a lot of penalties, so we had to be mindful of that.

Robbie talked about the position we, as a team, had put ourselves in. We had to win five in a row from that point: 'If we lose, we're gone. It's a life sentence. There is too much capability in this room.'

We heard from 1987 Wallabies captain Andrew Slack, who said he only thought about their missed opportunity 'every second day' now, and Robbie had been putting the message across: carpe diem—seize the day. It was there to be done and we believed we had the ability, we just had to execute it on the field.

I did a small amount of rehab running with the physios in the week leading up to the USA game. My back was feeling a bit better. I still didn't think I had any chance of playing that weekend, which was pretty disappointing. I had been looking forward to playing against the Americans. I remember in 2007 watching when the USA played South Africa and Takudzwa Ngwenya scored an amazing try that started with a Todd Clever intercept. From there they spun it to the other side of the field. Ngwenya had the outside on Habana and he burnt him down the sideline to score. It was an extraordinary try. I've heard stories about Takudzwa from 'The Beast'—all fellow Zimbabweans— but I hadn't met him and had never played against him, so I was really looking forward to that. But it wasn't to be.

A highlight away from rugby in Wellington was when Em and I caught a bus out to Newtown to visit a guy we'd met through Marty from Blackstar Coffee in Brisbane. His name is Matt and he was the inspiration for Marty starting Blackstar. It was great to see how he ran things. We also met his wife Beccy and their one-year-old son Archer, who was starting to walk—while we were there he took his second lot of unassisted steps, so that was cool to be a part of.

That afternoon I did some homework on the referee and put some footage on the computers showing how he refereed different aspects of the game. I also put a board up in the team room with some points about his refereeing—ensuring I still held up my usual off-field contribution despite not being able to be part of the main preparation.

I had a good catch-up with Sharpie in Wellington. It was really good just to sit down and chat. It's important to spend time with the guys. Even though you're in the team environment, it doesn't mean you're always hanging out away from training. But it's those kinds of relationships that really mean a lot—the ones where you hang out and have a chat about more than just rugby.

After tea with Sharpie (I'm not a huge tea drinker but he loves the stuff—maybe it is an age thing?), I went up and spent some more time in the hotel spa. The heat was good for my back, so I spent quite a bit of time in the spa over those few days. I'm really not a big fan of spas, spa baths or Jacuzzi-style bathing, but it was actually quite therapeutic. You just sit there in silence with yourself. One of the days I sat in there for quite a while and had a bit of a chuckle thinking about Canno and how much he sat in spas—the hot spa, definitely not the cold one—back at the Force. It was nice to think back to where it all started for me. It seemed like a really long time ago, but it wasn't really. I guess that's the thing you hear retired players say over and over again—you have to make the most of it while you're playing because one day it all ends and you often don't have control over how or when it ends.

That period of reflection made me more determined to make the most of my career. Being injured only enhanced that perspective even more. I really treasure the time I have playing for the Wallabies. I was reminded of the enormity of the opportunity I had playing at the Rugby World Cup. Despite having made it a lot harder for ourselves from that point on, the opportunity was still there to be taken and I was definitely keen to do absolutely everything I could to make it happen.

Wellington came alive on game day against the USA with a lot of people with Kiwi accents dressed as American supporters and also quite a few vocal Aussie fans. There was a group of fifty or so people outside the hotel to cheer the players as they boarded the bus to the ground, and in the stadium there was a mix of people dressed in Aussie gold or the American flag.

I was pretty nervous—I tend to get nervous on game day, even when I'm not playing. The guys not playing (the 'double dirties') were sitting pretty high up in the stands. We kept ourselves busy before the game reading all the signs people had in the crowd: 'Dingo stole my baby!', 'It's time to neuter Cooper', and one that a few female American supporters were holding, 'We slept with Tiger too'. The Wellington crowd certainly knows how to party and at times it seemed to be more concerned about the Mexican wave than the rugby.

We had a bit of a shaky start but then got moving, with Adam Ashley-Cooper eventually getting a hat trick and the Man-of-the-Match award. The guys secured the all-important bonus-point victory, despite some fairly strong resistance from USA early on. The match was really physical throughout and the worst part was that we picked up quite a few more injuries—Cliffy Palu pulled his hamstring and would play no further part in the tournament, Rob Horne suffered a fractured cheekbone, Pat McCabe dislocated his shoulder and Ant Faingaa was knocked out cold. Kurtley also suffered a hamstring strain and that would see him out for at least a week.

We were so stretched after injuries that our reserve hooker for that day, Stephen Moore, found himself on the wing at one point. After the game, he told me that after he got onto the field the first call was a cross-field kick. Clearly Quade hadn't realised he had a hooker on the wing.

Ant Faingaa was knocked out in an ugly tackle in the seventy-ninth minute, when he got his head caught in the wrong place. Both non-twenty-two playing groups were on the sideline when this happened and I was talking to Todd Clever, the usual captain for the USA, who they had rested to be fresh for the Italy game, and he was just as concerned as I was. It might be brutal on the field, but off the field there is very little animosity and you never want to see anyone get injured. Ant didn't move after being hit and it seemed like a long time before his motionless body eventually regained consciousness.

The medical team gave him a few words to remember and asked him to recite them every now and then. He was back in the change room and Robbie was asking Ant what the words were. Ant couldn't remember one of them. Digby Ioane and James O'Connor were trying to remember them too because they had been there when the Doc had asked him ten minutes earlier. The word was 'cat', but James said he was sure it was 'pat'.

'Mate, are you concussed too?', Digby joked.

Then Robbie chimed in: 'It's all that crap he puts in his hair that's frying his brains.'

We all had a good laugh at James's expense.

We were battered and bruised a lot more than we expected after the USA game, but they were the cards we were dealt and our resolve— and depth across the squad to cover for injuries—would be tested even further.

# 15.

# A Welcome Relief
## My return against Russia and victory over the Springboks

I t felt like there was an added tension and nervousness among the squad after losing to Ireland and I think to a large extent that was a positive thing. It was something that we needed to manage. The bottom line was that if we lost another game we were out, so there was good reason for the nerves. Nerves are not a bad thing—it's just how you manage them that matters most.

Although it was frustrating not to play in the USA game, I really enjoyed the week in Wellington. We had some nice time with one of Em's best friends, Rachel, who now lives there and is getting married to a Wellington local. I also enjoyed the extra time I was able to spend with my parents.

Mum and Dad loved their time travelling through rural New Zealand, but they were not enjoying some of the treatment Australians were getting. I said that if they insisted on wearing Wallabies' colours at all times, they would probably cop a bit of heat. But they reckon it was a bit too much, particularly in the stadiums with Kiwis supporting teams against Australia, cheering Wallaby mistakes, and abusing Wallaby supporters after the loss to the Irish. The Irish fans were apparently very gracious, but the Kiwis supporting Ireland went a bit overboard. All Blacks fans are passionate and it's to be expected. There was a lot of expectation and feeling at this World Cup for New Zealand and you could feel that among the people.

Another fun afternoon I had in Wellington was with Nick Phipps and James O'Connor—hanging out, passing a rugby ball while walking the streets and doing all sorts of flick passes between traffic signs, across roads and other things that my mum might not have been totally happy about. The ball nearly got run over only a few times. At one point a bus driver came to a complete stop to allow me to quickly grab the ball, before he smiled and continued on. I also managed to grubber the ball off the wharf and into the water at the busy Wellington waterfront. We stood there on a bridge watching the ball float out to sea, with a Springbok fan laughing at us and telling us not to get too upset about it. Then two schoolgirls came under the bridge in one of those foot-pedal boats and they were kind enough to retrieve the ball. It certainly saved me having to swim for it or buy James a new one.

I had a great skype with Luke O'Keefe from Wellington. We had decided to put the boot idea on hold for a moment so we could focus on the rugby balls and other sporting apparel. This would hopefully build a bit of capital and we could then spend the time and energy that's required to develop a quality football boot.

In the meantime we were looking at trying to get fair-trade sports balls into schools and sports clubs in Australia. Many major ball manufacturers use some very poor employment practices and we see this as a way of helping people that make those products. The fair-trade certification—apart from paying people a living wage—has a premium added to the cost, which the community uses for health-care, education, or areas that the community decides will be of greatest benefit. For example, in Pakistan, this premium has been used as a sort of insurance scheme, providing loans to begin rebuilding after the floods. It was a little something for us to keep ideas ticking and move towards making EightyTwenty a more self-sustaining entity, and in the process it would provide alternatives for consumers in Australia, improving the livelihoods of producers in third-world countries.

That week in Wellington was enjoyable right until the end. In the airport waiting to board our flight for Christchurch, Luke Burgess and I were looking in the comedy section of a music and DVD shop. Luke's eyes lit up when he spotted a limited edition copy of the iconic Australian film *The Castle*.

'I'm going to get this for Barnsey,' he joked. Berrick Barnes walked past. By the time we caught up with Berrick he was sticking his hand up the rear end of a sheep at a shop that sold New Zealand-made clothes. When you put your hand up there the sheep makes all sorts of 'baa-ing' sounds and even talks. It was quite amusing to all of the people walking past and sitting at the coffee shop not far from the shop. 'Happy birthday mate,' Luke said as he tossed the DVD to Berrick, laughing at how good his idea had been.

Berrick was delighted with his gift and it came in very handy on the team bus trip from Christchurch to Hanmer Springs, where we were all looking forward to the weekend off. Hanmer Springs is in the mountains about an hour-and-a-half north of Christchurch. The town is built alongside some natural hot springs and was settled in the 1800s. It's a beautiful little town that supports a good tourist industry as well as the local farming community, and it is a favourite haunt for Robbie Deans.

Robbie loves jet boating. He organised a bunch of his mates to bring their boats to Hanmer and players' and partners were taken for rides. It was so good to see Robbie relaxed and enjoying being out on the water. The team wasn't allowed to go in the boats because of liability issues, but I was happy just to watch and chat to people on the river bank.

Te Mania Angus Stud provided beef that was put on a spit and it tasted amazing. Another mate of Robbie's brought a bunch of crayfish. It was a huge lunch. Our partners made the trip to the river, and my parents and brother Steve were also invited, which was great. It was definitely one of the best things I've ever done on a rugby tour in terms of activities and meeting people. My dad spent his time chatting to farmers and even exchanged numbers with one of them. He said later how good it was to meet such amazing people and it definitely broke his prejudice against Kiwis after the verbal abuse he and Mum had copped in Auckland and Wellington.

We had dinner that Sunday night with Mum, Dad and Steve at the local pub and then they set off to Christchurch in time for Dad's flight back to Brisbane. All day, Em had been saying she hoped it would snow. Having grown up in the north of Western Australia she had hardly experienced a southern Australian winter, let alone seen snow. Sure enough, when we walked out of the pub after dinner that night it started snowing. We walked home in the snow and then Em stood outside for ten minutes saying, 'Dave, it's snowing! It's really snowing!' For the rest of the night she kept getting up to see if it was still snowing. It didn't snow very heavily but when we woke in the morning there was enough for her to maintain her excitement. It was a great few days at Hanmer Springs and on the Monday night in our villa Em and I cooked and I savoured my first home-cooked meal since getting to New Zealand. The simple things can become so special when you are on tour.

By Tuesday we were well and truly back in full swing with training and looking ahead to both the Russia game and a likely quarter-final against South Africa. We looked at our performance against USA and came up with a game plan for Russia. It was a fairly basic plan that would effectively set the foundation for us to expand upon for the quarter-final, keeping a bit up our sleeves to pull out for the Springboks game a week later. The Russian team had played with a lot of spirit in their earlier games and, despite not getting a win, they had played some good rugby and scored some impressive tries, so we definitely gave them the respect they deserved.

On the Tuesday afternoon we had an open training session and the locals turned out in numbers to watch. A busload of First XV players from northern Canterbury and Christchurch also trained with us during the warm-up passing games, and then held pads for the training session. After training we had a twenty-minute question-and-answer session where anyone could ask questions. A lot of them were directed at Robbie. The man is legendary in Canterbury, especially in the north of the province where the Deans family farm is located. The grocer in Hanmer Springs had a t-shirt in the shop window that said 'Robbie walks on water'. On the morning we left for Christchurch, it had been replaced with an All Blacks jersey.

We spent Wednesday in the most effected parts of Christchurch. After the devastating earthquakes, the community was dealt another blow as they missed out on hosting any Rugby World Cup games. Our team has a strong link with the city through Robbie, and our performance analyst Andrew Sullivan and media manager Matt McIlraith are also from Christchurch. We were initially scheduled to be based in Christchurch for the pool stages, so we felt it was the least we could do to bring a little bit of World Cup to this amazing community.

We were taken for a drive around the perimeter of the 'red zone' and saw the destruction from the quake and the demolition and reconstruction efforts. It was devastating, the sheer scale of the damage and destruction. One building had most of its windows boarded up, but a few still had glass and one had 'HELP' written on it from the inside. It's hard to comprehend how difficult it must be for the Christchurch community in those circumstances, so we were all more than willing to give up some of our time to spend with the people and keep them connected with the tournament.

From Christchurch it was on to Nelson, where we arrived on the Wednesday evening before our final pool match on the Saturday. I spent a while that night going through Russia's games at the tournament so far, and making sure I knew our game plan well. We had a few new set-ups off lineouts and some new patterns since I was out injured, so I made sure I was completely across all of that.

As the weekend drew near you could sense there was a real intensity in the group in training and meetings. The team for the Russia match was announced by our manager Bob Edgerton at a morning meeting on the Thursday and there were a few changes. Berrick Barnes was starting at inside centre, I was named at openside, Drew Mitchell was on the wing with Radike Samo on the other wing. Radike had trained a bit on the wing earlier that week, and until he was named I didn't quite believe he would actually play there. I was pretty happy to be in the starting team after two weeks out injured. I had had a chat to Robbie the night before and he said I'd start but it's such a good feeling hearing your name called out—something I'll never get used to or take for granted.

On Friday we had the captain's run at Trafalgar Park in Nelson. It was a smaller stadium than we usually played Test matches at, seating eighteen thousand people with a lot of temporary stands, but I really liked it. It felt like the stadium the Western Force plays at in Perth.

That week Dan Vickerman was out of the squad with a bit of an injury to his leg, so he was asked to present the jerseys after the team lunch. David Nucifora introduced him, having coached Dan when he played with the University of Queensland colts in the second row with Sharpie in 1996 before heading back to South Africa. He returned to Australia in 2000, and eventually worked his way into the Wallabies, debuting as Wallaby number 777. You could sense a bit of emotion in the room when he started to talk about how much the opportunity meant to him. Dan is such a passionate person and puts everything into what he does—you don't see him doing anything half-heartedly. He'll tell you himself that he wears his heart on his sleeve, which sometimes causes intense disagreements in the group, but his passion is really appreciated by everyone. All the boys love running out onto the field with him and oppositions must hate playing him because he charges into rucks and tackles with little regard for his two-metre plus frame.

I woke up on game day with the usual nerves. I hadn't played for two weeks, so I was a bit nervous about getting back into it and my back holding up. You can't afford to be worrying about injuries during the game, so I spent some time thinking about it beforehand, dealing with the mental aspect. I felt like I was good to go and was very excited about getting out there again.

By 2PM we were on the bus to the ground. For 8PM games we usually only have our team gathering and pre-game meal at 3PM, so this was a welcome change. I think afternoon games are fantastic—you usually get to play in sunny conditions that aren't too cold and you don't have to sit around all day.

We knew we had to come out firing. Despite not having won a game in their first Rugby World Cup, the Russians had fought hard and scored some great tries. We came out and blew them off the park in the first forty minutes, with the score 47–5 at the half-time break. I loved being out there again and enjoyed a bit more running with the ball through the new patterns we had. I managed to get over for two tries and Ben McCalman scored his first Test try, which I was pretty excited about. I think he was pretty surprised when I jumped up on him to celebrate the try, given that he got a gift pass from Quade with the line open. That was irrelevant in myy mind though—Ben works so hard in games and it was great to see him get over the line.

I got into the change room at the break and was so keen to play a bit more. Before the game, Robbie had said that he would keep me on for 'however long it takes to get a result'. I suspected he might tell me that I was done for the day, so I tried to avoid him a bit until I could say to our strength and conditioning coach that I needed a bit more of a run for my fitness. But Robbie was having none of it. 'You're done,' he said. 'Nice work.'

I watched the rest of the game from the bench. I knew the next weekend would be a massive game, so my mind wandered a few times to that fixture. The Russia game ended up 68–22. There weren't as many injuries to report compared with the USA game, but Drew Mitchell tore his hamstring picking up a ball on the fly. It was awful to watch. There was a gasp from the bench. We all know how good Drew is—he adds so much to the team on and off the field, his finishing is amazing and the forwards love seeing the ball torpedo off his left boot downfield to get us out of our end. We also knew he worked incredibly hard to make the World Cup after breaking his ankle during the Super Rugby season. Now his tournament was over.

Drew's injury definitely dampened the mood in the change room after the game. We had won with a bonus point, securing our place in the quarter-finals. But Drew was heading home and we were sad for him. He seemed to deal with the initial disappointment well and just sat there taking it in.

I had media duties on the Sunday morning after our victory over Russia. The big news was that All Blacks star Dan Carter was out of the tournament after injuring his groin at kicking training. You never wish injury on anyone and can't help but feel for guys who get injured like that. They have all worked so hard to get to the tournament and it must be heartbreaking to have the opportunity taken away.

I had lunch with Emma, Mum and Steve before they drove to Picton to catch the ferry across to Wellington. Mum and Steve flew back to Brisbane. They had knitting needles and wool at the cafe we had lunch at and Mum showed me how to knit. My gran taught me on the farm back in Zimbabwe but I had forgotten. It was quite funny. I thought I might get some knitting needles when I get home and have a go at making a scarf for when we travel over to New Zealand again.

Nelson was a really nice place, but after the rain started in the second half of the Russian game it didn't stop for the remaining time we were there. There were plenty of jokes about it being 'the sunniest place in New Zealand'. We had to spend Sunday night in Nelson because we were not sure which quarter-final we were playing in until Ireland and Italy played out the final match of our pool.

Ireland won against Italy to finish first in our pool, so that confirmed we would play South Africa in the Sunday quarter-final in Wellington. In Wellington on the Monday preparations began in earnest for what was going to be the biggest match most of us had ever played in. We had a strategy meeting that ended up lasting about three hours. We tried to look at every aspect of our game and how we could best play South Africa. By the end we had a comprehensive document that would be presented to the group on Tuesday morning after our review of the Russian game.

After a mini-team dinner on the Monday I headed out to stay the night with Em in the campervan. It was pretty fun with the pull-out bed in the kitchen, and the rain thundering against the windows. It was a welcome break from staying in hotels, even if just for a night.

On the Tuesday morning I had medicals followed by the team review and preview. We made sure everyone was clear about the way that we wanted to train that week and play against the Springboks. Robbie told the group, 'We are going to do this.' He stressed the importance of preparing well and being in the moment and connected with our team mates: 'You will think of these moments for the rest of your days and you will cherish them for what you brought to the team and what the team did together.' After the meeting the forwards walked through our lineout options.

There is a good energy in the group. Luke 'Burgo' Burgess had been really hyper—and he is hyper most of the time, so when I say that I mean he was non-stop high energy. I was rooming with Adam Ashley-Cooper and Burgo was trying to get into the room to wrestle. Adam and I had wrestled him and Berrick in their room earlier and they came back for another showdown. We knew they would. There was a knocking on the door and the peephole had a finger over it. 'Coopy' had the foresight to put the door lock on before turning the handle. Burgo launched himself against the door but came to a very sudden stop after it had opened ten or so centimetres as the chain lock caught on. Burgo was making growling noises. We were in hysterics as he growled and howled like a dog or some other sort of creature. Adam grabbed a bottle of water and sprayed him with water. It was a good shot and got him right in the mouth, so we could hear Luke spluttering out in the hallway. We had a good chuckle. That was the end of that.

I didn't watch much television during the tournament apart from a few of the games. The World Cup and just rugby in general seemed to be inescapable. The All Blacks were especially hard not to see on television. Every second advertisement was for something or other, so I avoided it. We have more than enough rugby just with the preparation and playing, so to sit back and see more rugby was too much. Em and I don't have pay television at home, and just have an old set my parents gave me when I moved out of home, so going without television is actually normal for me and particularly good considering we are spending so much time thinking, talking, training and playing rugby.

On the Thursday evening I had some nice time with Em and managed to get away from what had been a fairly intense week of preparation. We sat in a little cafe and did some work together, which was not particularly romantic but it was tough trying to find time to do the stuff I need to do for EightyTwenty. We were progressing with the rugby ball idea. The quality was not particularly good at the start of the process, but we've been working with the manufacturer to produce a higher quality match ball and we're developing a marketing strategy to sell them. It's pretty small start but it is exciting. We will sell them under the Heroes Boots brand as we slowly keep moving towards our goal of having a rugby boot that is made in a workers co-operative or fair-trade certified factory.

Wellington was abuzz with lots of fans as the weekend drew near. On the Friday we had a really sharp field session. Everyone was so enthusiastic, but we also brought a lot of precision and executed well. We worked a lot on receiving high balls from the Springboks and kicks in behind us, and also worked on our defence and attacking patterns and phase plays. We had a real sense of urgency and also excitement about the upcoming game.

The team was announced on the Friday morning before our Sunday match and there were no real surprises. It was great to have Pat McCabe back at inside centre. The physios and medical team had done a good job working on his shoulder and his go-forward in the midfield would be important for our game plan. My roommate (and wrestling partner) for the week, Adam Ashley-Cooper, was named at outside centre, Digby Ioane was back on the wing and Kurtley Beale was also back from injury. Digby has one of the highest work-rates in the team, and Kurtley brings a huge skill set with the way he can take opportunities and bring himself into the line and counter-attack.

Once we were back at the hotel after a team dinner on Friday night I went over our strategy document again and wrote it all out once more, making sure I knew everything backwards. When you're under pressure and in the moment you don't want to have to think about detail. It needs to happen automatically.

After that Adam cut my hair. We'd been chatting about it for a few days and he'd set up a chair in the bathroom (his 'salon'). He spent a good half hour cutting it and shaping it. I had wanted a haircut for a while, so I was pretty happy to get one— especially from 'Swoop', who has to be one of the more stylish guys in the squad.

On the Saturday we woke up to rain outside and the wind was howling too. It made for some humorous times at training and the captain's run. A few of the boys kicked the ball a hundred metres during the warm-up—it just didn't stop rolling in the wind. We trained well and went through patterns and then lineouts, which were also quite comical. A straight throw to the middle of the lineout caught by the wind and landed five metres behind us. Another one flew out of line and hit me square on the side of the ear.

After training I fronted a press conference with James Horwill and Will Genia. I just sat there for the first five or ten minutes while questions were fired at the other two. My boyhood idol, Bob Skinstad, was in the press conference. I was hoping to have a chat afterwards but our media manager, Matt McIlraith, had told us to get out of there straight afterwards.

I did some more video work on South Africa that Saturday afternoon and then headed out of the hotel with Em for an hour or two. I was keen to feel the vibe in Wellington. There was a fair buzz around by that time with a lot of vibrant Irish and Welsh supporters on their way to the stadium for their quarter-final clash.

On the Saturday night I hung out with a dozen or so guys in the team room, watching Ireland against Wales. Wales played a great game to defeat Ireland, with their centres making inroads and their team defence outstanding. By the end of that match I was starting to really feel the nerves so I went for a spa and stretch and then looked at footage of Springboks openside flanker Heinrich Brussow and his running lines to breakdowns. He was going to be a tough opponent and I wanted to be sure I was ready for how he would play the game.

That night I dreamt about rugby, and woke up on the Sunday to vague memories of some game I was involved in just in time for physio and a stretch. I had a quick coffee with Em and Dad, who had flown in the night before.

We had a team meeting and went through strategy and anything anyone was unsure of. Then it was time for strapping. We had another brief team meeting at which Robbie talked about playing like men. He said only men win tournaments like this and we had to do everything it took to get a result. We knew we could do it and we were the only ones who could now.

I got goosebumps as we walked through the hotel lobby to the bus. The place was going crazy with people packed in to see us onto the bus. They were singing 'Waltzing Matilda' and someone was playing bagpipes. There were so many people that no one else could fit into the lobby and they were crowded outside on the pavement and spilling out onto the street. If it hadn't yet hit us, this definitely drove home just how important this match was to Australian rugby fans.

I was very nervous. This was the knockout stage of a World Cup. In the afternoon I had sat on my bed and thought how I got here—my love of the game, which had started in Zimbabwe, and then training so hard to realise my goals. Getting up at 5:30AM to go to the gym or do fitness or hill runs in our cul-de-sac before school; getting up early on holidays to get my training done before everyone was out and about so I could enjoy the day with the family. I had made it to this point, but there was no more to do. The game was there to be won.

The day before the game Chris 'Buddha' Handy presented the jerseys and talked about how much it meant to him to be a Wallaby and how special it was in his life to see his mother cry tears of joy because he had realised his goal, something he had worked hard for. Buddha is known for a good jersey presentation—having famously presented the jerseys with a stirring speech to the Wallabies before the 1999 final against France. He talked about how unconditional his mother's love was and that was why it was so special, because they don't care whether you come first or last, you are still their baby. But to see your mum react in a certain way when you achieve something was that little bit more special. He asked us to think about our mums and how special they were and how much they had put into our lives in their own way.

It was one of the better jersey presentations and he had the attention of everyone, with a few teary eyes as he talked with so much passion. I decided to dedicate the game to my mum and thought about her a lot in the preparation. She has sacrificed so much in her life to help us grow into the men we wanted to be. She has laughed with me, cried with me and encouraged me. She always joins in our adventures and she's such a good friend to all three of us as well as being our mum. Even when I was grumpy or tired or injured, she was always so patient and loving—she really has taught me so much about how to love someone consistently and truly. She's the glue in our family and she is an amazing mother.

Mum wasn't able to be at the match—she was back in Brisbane with my brothers Mike and Steve. The family finances have been tight since Dad has gone back to full-time university to do his Masters in counselling, something that he is brilliant at and has wanted to do for a long time. So Mum was working full-time and flew back to get back to work after the game against Russia—yet another example of how amazing she is and continues to be for our whole family.

We never really got into the quarter-final. We had a few chances but they came to little, apart from early on when I managed to get my boot on a ball in a ruck and kick it out to Radike. He picked it up and passed it out to James Horwill, who crashed over for our only try. We defended for what seemed like most of the game. Being in defence for so long is tiring, but the fact that we weren't giving away too many penalties and were able to force a few turnovers gave us the lift we needed to hold on. When they hit the lead in the second half it took a lot to get down their end and get a penalty, which James O'Connor did well to knock over and put us back in the lead. We could sense that we were almost there and it was a huge relief when the final whistle blew. We had done it and found a way to win despite a somewhat poor team performance. We had advanced to the semi-finals. The dream was still alive.

I was really happy to be named man of the match and after the game I had to do a lot of media—four television interviews followed by two radio interviews. When I finally made it back to the change room it was fairly lively, but nothing over the top. The guys were enjoying sitting back and chatting, getting some fluids in and peeling off the strapping tape. I love the atmosphere in the change room after a win, laughing and joking about moments in the game and just enjoying the moment with the guys you've just worked so hard with.

Robbie talked to us one more time for closure and then Buddha came back for a few words about how proud he was of us. We then sang the national anthem, as is customary when we win, before Will Genia and Digby Ioane took control of the music and kept the R&B coming thick and fast. We knew we had done well to win the game. We had done it the hard way, without the ball and at the wrong end of the field for much of the game, but that didn't detract anything from the feeling in the change room.

Then it was back to the hotel. We watched the All Blacks v Argentina game in the team room with family and friends—I had some family there too as Dad, Em and her parents, John and Jenny, joined us. They all went home after the match apart from Em, so we hung out while I iced in the physio room. My shoulder was sore and I had copped a cork on my quad just above my knee, so I hooked myself up to the attachments that allow the icing machine to pump cold water through the sleeves around my shoulder and leg. There were a few other boys taking turns on the ice machines. Kurtley was icing his hammy, Ben Alexander a cork on his quad, Sekope his ankle and Pat McCabe his shoulder.

Eventually, at about 1AM, I decided to head back to the campervan to get some sleep. My Dad and Em were staying in there, and it was only a short walk from the hotel. It didn't take long to get to sleep, but at about 3AM I woke up with my shoulder aching, so I walked back to the hotel to ice it until the medicals at 8AM in the morning.

Kurtley and Sekope were still in the physio room on mattresses on the floor, fast asleep, so I pulled what I thought was a bed over next to Keps in an effort to share his ice machine and put it on my shoulder. I was set. I had my shoulder hooked up, turned the machine on, and then collapsed onto the bed—but it was just a base and the wooden slats were hard, thudding into my ribs. I had to laugh. In the dark I hadn't seen that there wasn't a mattress, it was just a base. I was pretty tired so I ended up just falling asleep on the floor in the medical room with the ice machine hooked up to my shoulder, and was woken up when the doctor and physios came in for the medicals.

After medicals I had breakfast with Dad and Em, and Sharpie and Steve Moore joined us before the barista shouted us a round of coffees. My Twitter feed was going crazy with abuse from people about me 'cheating'. After the game people started saying I had cheated against the South Africans with my play at the breakdown. It's a pretty common claim to be leveled at an openside flanker. Sometimes it happens because people don't understand the rules at the breakdown or they feel like the referee is missing things. I didn't read much of it and decided to try and avoid it. There were obviously a lot of disappointed people after the game and they were entitled to voice their opinions. It was my choice to use Twitter, so there is no reason for me to get upset about it. I hadn't read any articles in the newspapers either, but my dad said there was a lot of negative press about Bryce Lawrence's performance. It must be a tough gig being a referee—you can never please everyone. I think Bryce is a good referee and all the players would have had him many times during the Super Rugby season, so his style was nothing new to either team. I thought he was pretty consistent during the game—where he didn't blow that much at the tackle contest and allowed both teams to have a go at the ball—but it obviously didn't help the Springboks that their 'fetcher', Heinrich Brussow, had left the field after twenty minutes. It certainly opened up the breakdown contest for me to capitalise and I was glad that I did.

# 16.

# A Temporary Ending
## Semi-final loss will make us better for next time

After a long night of icing injuries after our Springbok victory, we made our way to Auckland. There was a week of preparation ahead of us before the semi-final against the All Blacks—what a week it was to come. We were staying out of the city on the north shore. I had never stayed there before, but apparently it is home to most of Auckland's one hundred thousand South African migrants so it promised to be an interesting week, especially given how much banter we were copping from South African supporters after beating the Boks in the quarter-final.

The focus for Monday was recovery and after a late lunch we were back on the bus to a pool and recovery centre in Auckland. I was still so tired and sore and really just needed to sleep to give my body time to rest.

I had a big sleep-in on the Tuesday before physio and medicals at 10AM. Our physios—Andrew and James—and Warren, the team doctor, had been flat out on this trip and always seemed to be treating someone when you walked past their room. Warren is on call at any time of the day or night. He is such a caring person that you can't help but feel like everything is going to be ok when you sit down to sort out a problem with him.

The Springboks game was very physical and a lot of us were feeling it in our recovery. Looking back on the match, it felt like all we did was defend. It was great to get the win in the end, but I was very aware—as was most of the group—of how much we had to improve to beat the All Blacks. If we gave New Zealand that much ball, they have the firepower to score tries and punish teams that turn the ball over or kick it to them with space. South Africa did actually run it a lot more against us than they usually do, but luckily our defence was good enough and we were able to turn the ball over at crucial times.

I looked over the game and we had a bit of a team review. We also came together to come up with a strategy of how best to approach the All Blacks. Phil Blake gave such a passionate presentation before the South Africa game about their threats and ways to shut them down. He showed us how their big forwards back into contact and try to get offloads, so we knew what was coming. He also showed clips of us in defence shutting them down in previous games. Phil gets right into it. Once you have an understanding of the patterns and systems in place, he believes defence is all about 'attitude' and he loves his 'attitude drill'. It is basically a one-on-one tackle after both starting on the ground in a three by three metre square. One person is the attacker and the other is the defender. If you don't stop a try within three attacking plays you have to do extras after training.

During one of the Gold Coast camps before the World Cup, the team came up with a big list of things that could possibly derail our efforts. In a quick team meeting after the strategy session, Robbie reminded us of this list and said that one item from the list was about players seeking personal promotion above the team. It all seemed a bit serious when he said, 'This has come to my attention, and it's simply not good enough,' before putting up a photo on the projector of Nick Phipps, with the cheesiest grin, advertising an ice machine for the Melbourne Rebels. The room erupted in laughter and the boys had a good laugh at Nick's expense.

Nick has brought so much energy to the group despite being part of the eight that don't play most weeks. We dubbed them all the 'great eight' (and would write it as 'Gr8 8') to recognise the positive effect they have on the team's preparations and how this affects the lead up to games. The great eight have been fantastic all tournament and Nick, in particular, has been so positive. He's always willing to help and trains so hard when the great eight do extra fitness or weights sessions. It's so important to have guys like that around who are working hard, so that when they do get an opportunity, they are ready. Matt Hodgson has also added a lot by being a pest at the breakdown when we are going through our attack at training. He keeps everyone honest and having Matt making sure we keep the focus on the breakdown is great preparation.

Our game plan was a lot simpler that week. We got through hardly any of the detail that we had trained in the game against South Africa, having to rely rather on our defence to get us through. But New Zealand are such a different team to play against, with a different way of defending to South Africa, so you have alter the way you play slightly to deal with this defence. While the South African centres are very good at shooting out of the line to shut off attack and generating line speed, the Kiwis generally give you space on the outside and then drift hard to close it. It's very tempting to think that you can just go wide, but the space closes very quickly. They get you over the touch line or contest that breakdown hard when you are short in numbers and they are coming across.

We had a press conference on the Wednesday and it was the biggest one I have ever been at. James O'Connor, myself, James Horwill, Rocky and Quade fronted up. The questions ended up being very entertaining, with a few about the breakdown in the South African game, then a lot about the pressure on Quade and the crowd's reactions to him. Every time he gets the ball, in every game we played in New

Zealand, there were huge 'boos' from the crowd. There were also a lot of questions about his 'poor match' against South Africa. Quade was great and said he would rather he have a bad game and the team win than play his best game and we lose.

A journo asked James O'Connor about 'scissors, paper, rock' and how he'd tweeted that he had won Saia's lunch money. The journalist challenged him to a game—she was very attractive, so the crowd of mostly male journalists didn't seem too phased by this (I would have liked to have seen a middle-aged man try the same stunt). Much to James' horror she beat him! Our media manager, Matty Mac, was quick to say, 'Ok, thanks for that, but now back to the rugby questions.'

That afternoon, five of us went to the spa instead of doing weights and afterwards I watched our game against South Africa again. There were still so many little things I could improve on and there were opportunities for the team to improve as well. But those opportunities excited me. I also looked at the All Blacks starter plays they used this World Cup, particularly in the last game against Argentina. They used Ma'a Nonu a lot and Piri Weepu seems to have a lot more involvement to make up for the loss of Dan Carter.

For dinner, we split into groups. In the team room, five columns had been drawn up on the board, with five different categories. We had to put our names in the category we most thought we fitted. The categories were: graziers, entertainers, on the tools, banking and finance, and industrialists. I put myself in the 'graziers' group, for guys with a connection to the land. Joining me in the group was 'Farmer' Sharpe, Rocky, Ben McCalman, Simmo and James Slipper. The entertainers were Luke Burgess, Berrick, Adam, Quade, Taf, and Salesi. The 'on the tools' group was Diggers, Willy G, Sekope, Hodgo and Radike. Banking and finance was Dan, Pat, Lachie, Kurtley, James O'Connor and Nick. And the industrialists had Steve Moore, James Horwill, Rob Horne, Benny A, Ant F and Scott Higginbotham.

We had a great night out at a Vietnamese place, which Sharpie had been to before. We asked the waitress to order for us and the food just started coming. Then it stopped and the guys looked around and Rocky asked, 'Do any of you feel like you could eat just what we had, again?' Yes, we were still hungry, so we ordered more. Buffets at the hotel might seem extravagant but imagine if you had to try and feed thirty players plus staff at a restaurant every night?

In my spare time, I had been trying to organise flights to Zimbabwe and liaise with Luke and a cameraman who has offered to film our trip. The cameraman owns a film company and really believes in what we are doing—he also knows Anania who runs things in Nkayi, so we have that connection. There are always so many 'ifs' when planning around rugby—you never know if you'll be on Spring Tour or what will happen, but you have to organise the rest of your life and hope for the best. Our plan is to fly to Zimbabwe the day after the game against Wales in Cardiff, then straight to Nkayi for the week. I'm really looking forward to a holiday.

On the Thursday, Em and I sat at a café for a few hours to do some work. While we were there Ant Faingaa walked past the window and waved to us. Em started to say, 'I don't think I've ever seen him without Saia before,' but as she finished her sentence Saia walked past the window trailing Ant and talking on the phone. Watching the two of them I've often thought about what it must be like playing with your brother. Both Mike and Steve are pretty naturally gifted. Steve pursued his rugby until his back ruled him out—having played First XV at school and being signed up to the Force academy. Mike's never been that keen on playing anything except for fun—and, boy, does he make a tough 'social' competitor. Out of the three of us, he probably has the best coordination and reflexes, and I always try to avoid doing too much wrestling with Mike because he's so strong. Ant and Saia have the added bond of being twins but they also have a younger brother, Colby, who plays for the Brumbies, and another brother, Vili, who plays rugby league for the Ipswich Jets. Four boys in one family playing contact sport at that level sure must be tough on their Mum.

We had a really good training day on the Friday before the semi-final. We had a defensive preview with Phil Blake after our strategy meetings and he got right into it again. The team learnt a lot and enjoyed his passion.

I did some work on the referee that afternoon. Craig Joubert is a good referee and we've had him a number of times. I thought he was going to try and be strict on the breakdown after the media storm following our win against the Springboks, so I tried looking at the best ways to contest the breakdown without giving away penalties as I thought he would be looking for opportunities to penalise me early to try to set boundaries.

Between all of our match preparation and training commitments I managed to have a lot more communication with Luke O'Keefe about Heroes Boots. We sourced fair-trade rugby balls and Luke was setting up a website to sell my book and the balls on. We are hoping to get schools to start using fair-trade certified sports equipment—particularly schools that have inquired about EightyTwenty Vision and ways they can help. I'm keen to show people that there are so many ways the products we use are linked to third-world manufacturing processes. Just by changing the way we consume we can help people in developing countries. When more and more people start to realise this then this will lead to change in the way that people are treated in factories and workplaces the world over. So we are aiming to provide schools and clubs with customisable sporting equipment as a way to offer alternatives and at the same time use any profits to help people in need here in Australia and abroad. Hopefully, it will at least provide some income to start Heroes as a company and later provide EightyTwenty with a more steady income stream.

We had a really fun team dinner on the Friday night before the semi-final, which featured a 'poetry slam' in our mini groups. We have Berrick in our group and he has memorised a number of Australian poems and delivers them brilliantly, so I was sure he would do well. The highlight was a rap by Tatafu with backing music Digby 'DJ Rat' Ioane had made on his laptop. It was a really good laugh. Everyone was in good spirits despite the serious edge of the big game the next day.

Former Wallaby Jeff Sayle presented our jerseys at the captain's run and it was also very special to have legendary swimmer Dawn Fraser come along too and say a few words. Jeff gave a really energising talk about his philosophies about the game and what it meant to him.

Game day was such a long day. I had a decent sleep although I did battle to get to sleep at all. I couldn't stop thinking about the game. I got up, got out of the hotel at 10AM and saw my family, then was back at the hotel at about 12PM for some physio and lunch. I went to the pool and got chatting to some French supporters who had been to the French game against Wales. They were asking me if the Kiwi crowd was always so hostile and I said that, yes, they're pretty passionate about their rugby over here. The Frenchman told me that after they'd beaten Wales, the Kiwis had thrown beer cans at them—which I thought was pretty poor form. But I guess it's the usual story of a couple of idiots ruining it for everyone else and maybe you get that everywhere. Although they did say this would never happen in Europe and I guess they'd know.

After a brief stint in the spa I went back to my room. I thought I'd have a sleep, but instead I lay in bed for about three hours thinking about the game. I was feeling quite nervous—I usually do before games—and I was very restless and keen to just get on with it. Our team meeting was at 4:30PM for the pre-game meal and strapping, then at 7PM we had our pre-game gathering and headed off to the stadium.

There is little more I can say about the game except that we were beaten fair and square.

After the final whistle, I was shattered. It was over. We lost. We'd really failed to execute the way that we'd planned and the All Blacks managed to score that early try and then just keep the score board ticking over. We thanked the crowd because they'd been really good— well, the small pockets of Aussies in the crowd at least—then we made our way back to the change room. It was definitely the quietest change room I've ever been in. No one said a word. We all just sat staring into space and thinking about the game, about the missed opportunity. There were a few tears. A lot of work had gone into it and we'd come up short. It's very hard to describe.

We had high expectations of ourselves and this wasn't how we saw it ending. After what seemed like almost an hour—but it was probably only about twenty minutes—John O'Neill thanked us for our efforts and told us how proud he, the ARU and Aussies back home were of us and how important it was to pick ourselves up for the third place play-off on Friday night. Anthony Albanese had also come to the game as some sort of government representative and, to his credit, he just laid low in the corner and didn't try to talk to too many guys. He was very friendly when I went up to him to say gidday and have a chat after sitting at my locker for a good half an hour. I remember Kevin Rudd coming into a losing change room once and he was very similar in that no one was up for too much conversation or anything really and he also seemed to understand and respect that.

We slowly started to take off our strapping tape and shower and get changed. Robbie had spoken about how you really find out about the character of people when they win and lose, and how they are affected by that. He said we had to show our character by dealing with the loss and getting ourselves up for the game on Friday to end on a good note. It was our last chance, and for some it would be their last taste of World Cup rugby.

Will and I shared the man-of-gold award, which is apparently the first time it's ever been shared. While it's always nice to be recognised by the people you care about, your teammates, it was little consolation after the loss. While I don't think too many people in the rugby world care about the bronze final, we felt it was important for us to finish well.

We stayed out on the North Shore again in the week leading up to the bronze final. Not being in Auckland city, there was little World Cup hype. Leaving the hotel for the semi-final there wasn't the same support and buzz that we had enjoyed in Wellington.

I spent a lot of the Monday after the semi-final loss with Em and my family. I'd stayed out with Em on the Sunday night, so in the morning we headed back to Takapuna and had some breakfast before I had to go off for medicals and treatment. Then I went back to where my family was staying and Em cooked us all dinner. Her parents came over as well. They were flying out the next morning, so there were quite a few of us for dinner. It was really nice but by 8PM I was exhausted and keen to get to sleep.

The Tuesday team meeting was our first for the week and Robbie said that although we were all hurting we had to get up for the Wales game. He said we were all feeling 'hollow and gutted' that we let go of a chance that will never come back to us. 'We have to master the reasons why we didn't take that opportunity. We have to use it in such a way that we never have that hollow feeling in our guts again. We have to aspire to be the best in the world. There's first, and nowhere. Don't think about it from your own individual perspective, it's all about having the Wallabies win. It's time we stepped up to number one … from this moment every moment is a training moment. It goes like that,' and he clicked his fingers.

I felt gutted for a long time that week. Four years is a long time to work towards a goal and then have it vanish in eighty minutes.

On Wednesday before the bronze final, I woke up to the sound of rain crashing on the balcony and window. I headed downstairs for strapping before a bus ride to training at North Harbour Stadium. The rain stopped after a while and it was a really good session. The team was named before the training session. There were a few injuries, with Keps out after he copped a finger in the eye. Some guys claimed it was me, but I had no recollection of it in the game. My thumb was a bit sore—so hopefully it wasn't my thumb in his eye. Stephen Moore had hurt his sternum, Pat McCabe's shoulder was pretty sore and Dan Vickerman went back to Australia to have a plate removed from his leg. So Sharpie was in for his one hundredth game, which was pretty exciting for the big man.

Jonah Lomu had made contact with Robbie and wanted to catch up on the Wednesday, so Robbie invited him down to training. It was amazing to see the excitement about having him there. Digby walked passed him and Jonah said, 'Hey, Digby, how are you going?' and had a chat to him. Digby ran out the tunnel and onto the field and he was buzzing, saying how excited he was: 'Bro, he said my name! He said my name man! This has made my tournament!'

It was great to see and it's amazing the effect Jonah has on players with what he has achieved on the rugby field, the adversity that he has overcome and the problems he continues to face off the field with his kidney troubles. After training I went up and sat in the stand with him, Sekope, Quade and James and Jonah told us stories about when he used to play and what they got up to. He's a great storyteller and he had us in stitches. In the change room afterwards, we got a few photos with him and then we were back to the hotel. During a scrum meeting that day Patricio Noreiga said to us: 'In every moment you are writing history. Next year, you or I might not be here, but this team will. Enjoy it. You play a small part in this team, but the team continues with the history that you help create. Look at who you are and who you are representing and what your goals are.'

No one playing was allowed to do weights that afternoon because it was such a short turnaround. We just had physio and massage and I looked at footage on the computers. Em came in on Wednesday afternoon briefly between lunch and my physio appointment and we had a coffee together. She had been really busy having both our families in New Zealand and organising them all so it was nice to just have time to hang out together. Semi-final week was pretty crazy and this week had been busy too. We were nearing the end of it all and it was nice to just sit down and talk.

That evening we all met in the team room before we went to a players' dinner. Rocky had organised a slideshow of photos of Sharpie's career right from when he started at the Reds with a full head of hair till this World Cup. It was great to watch it together, and we could appreciate just how long he's been playing for. Rocky made his Test debut when I was fourteen, so to play with him was pretty special. Rocky had also managed to get former Wallaby hooker Michael Foley to send over a video congratulating Sharpie. Foles is the new Waratahs head coach and Sharpie played with him when they were in Queensland together. Foles also coached the Wallabies forwards for three years from 2006 to 2009, so they have had quite a long association. The video he sent contained a few embarrassing stories and then there was a video that Gits had sent over, which was very funny. After that Pat McCabe shared a poem he had written about Sharpie, and had the boys in stitches. Pat's a very good poet and he did a number of poems for the team this year.

On the Thursday we had our captain's run and jersey presentation by John Eales, it was pretty special. He asked us to think of four things leading up to the game; the first Test we ever saw; remember and reflect on our first Test and the emotions that brought; the unknown fan—a person we'd never thought of before; and someone who was really important in our career who had planted the seed. He also talked about thinking about our teammates, and ourselves, and the joy of the first and the fear of the last. John's an incredibly gifted speaker. He manages to communicate things in a way that is clear, succinct and inviting. And in that environment he has the credibility to support his message, which obviously makes the guys listen pretty carefully to what he has to say. There is a lot of respect in the group for past players, and we're all aware of how much we can learn from them—especially from someone like John Eales.

After that we had our captain's run, which was pretty sharp. With the short turnaround between the All Blacks game on Sunday and the Friday game, the coaching staff have been pretty careful not to overload us so we'll be fresh for the game. It's been a long tournament and a long year. We've all played a lot of rugby, so everyone is pretty fatigued and the coaching staff is trying to manage that to minimise injuries.

Robbie invited Jonah Lomu to join us for our team dinner the night before the game. He gave a bit of a talk at the dinner and said: 'People always remember you by your last game.' Which was poignant given that it was Luke Burgess's last game before heading to France and Sharpie's one hundredth test. Jonah talked a little about what life has been like for him over the past few months and he said he spent three weeks in hospital, fighting to survive. Then he went on to talk about the game. He told us to, 'Forget about third position overall—play for your pride and country. This is the hard time. This is when you find out the character of a team. The game comes first. The team comes first. Do the work on the field, and everything else will follow. If you go back to what got you starting the game, that's the key that people forget when they go professional. You have a guy who's played one hundred games at Test-match level. Mate, that makes me motivated to play for him. Don't doubt yourselves. Don't ever doubt yourselves.'

It was a timely message for us from an absolute legend of the game and a Rugby World Cup icon. During the week we had to nominate one thing we were going to play for and lots of the boys said their drive to win was for Sharpie. In close games those kinds of things can make all the difference. Nathan was the captain at the Force right from the very start and I had grown up watching him play. He made his test debut when I was fourteen, which was hard for me to get my head around. During our time in Perth I've been able to get to know him pretty well. As well as being a brilliant player and a great leader in the team, Sharpie is just a really good man and really great mate. It was brilliant to have someone like Jonah, who has done so much both on and off the field, remind us that we play for each other and we play for the team and for the privilege of the opportunity to be wearing the Wallabies jersey. So even though we'd rather have been playing on Sunday night there was a renewed energy and excitement in the group for the challenge ahead.

I slept in until about 9.30AM on game day ahead of the bronze final. Em came in to meet me and we went for a coffee and a walk. Then she was meeting up with Jess, Sharpie's wife, and their two boys who had flown in the night before, so I went and tried to have a bit of a sleep. Since the games are played so late, it makes it a long day so I've had to try and fill up my time and have a few naps—otherwise it's easy to become agitated waiting to head off for the stadium. We had our usual team gathering at about 4:30PM—Quade said that we could have all the detail in the world, have all the right plays and patterns and things in place, but it was all worthless and meant nothing if we didn't turn up in the right frame of mind to play positively and want to use the ball. We were in game mode. We had strapping and our meal and another quick team meeting and then it was onto the bus and off to the stadium.

We knew Wales would come out firing. They were a young team too, and bronze would mean a lot to them after their loss to the French. We had talked about using the ball and playing and that's how we started the game, trying to use the ball and even taking a quick tap when the three points were on offer. Momentum shifted when Quade and Kurtley got injured almost at the same time, with Kurtley re-tearing his hamstring and Quade tearing his anterior cruciate ligament. Berrick Barnes did well when he moved in to No. 10 to direct traffic but we didn't threaten their line like we did in the first ten or so minutes.

Defensively they were one of the better teams at the tournament and they scramble well when you get in behind them. It was a real arm wrestle for most of the game after the early try from Berrick—he sliced through from a scrum off a great ball from Quade.

It was very physical and both teams threw themselves into it, with a number of players spending time in the blood bin. I had to get my head bandaged a few times after getting a cut in a ruck. I have no idea how it happened, and only knew about it when referee Wayne Barnes told me I needed to get off for a blood bin. I had blood streaming down my face, but told him it could be fixed up very quickly as there was no way I wanted to go off given the injuries we'd already had and how tight the game was. The doc and physio taped it up and I was back into it. Wayne is a very good referee and his laid-back approach is appreciated by the players. He never seems to get flustered and talks a lot during the game, allowing players to react before he penalises, which helps the flow of the game. Shane Williams, in possibly his last games for Wales, showed his class to score off a grubber in behind us by their halfback.

Things got pretty intense and there was a bit of push and shove at one point. One of their players said to me, 'I'll knock your head off next time.' Will Genia burst out laughing and said, 'I'd really like to see you try.' It was such a funny moment in the heat of it all, and we had a good laugh about it after the game. When James Horwill and Will went off I took over the captaincy, although I didn't really realise it and change too much about how I went about things. We didn't have to say much, we knew what we had to do: defend well and then hold onto the ball when we got it.

We did enough to win it, kicking a few penalties to give us a lead, and then Ben McCalman scored to put us more than a converted try ahead. To their credit, Wales kept attacking and eventually scored two minutes into injury time after twenty-plus phases. Both teams were exhausted, and no doubt relieved that it was over. We had come third and managed to finish with a win. The other option was unthinkable.

There was a lot of emotion about it being Sharpie's one hundredth and how much he has given to Australian rugby. His family were there and it was special to see his two sons on the field with him after the game and then in the change room, running around with bronze medals around their necks. Sharpie was presented with his one hundredth cap, a few of the boys spoke about what it meant to play with him and he was given a few gifts, including a bottle of Grange from the year he made his debut—which, true story, had to be bought from a museum, much to the delight of all the boys.

I woke up at about 10:30AM on the Saturday. We had a team meeting at 12pm and then most of the boys were heading home at 1pm. I could have gone home, but I had to be at the IRB awards ceremony on the Monday night with a few of the other boys and it just seemed ridiculous to go back to Perth and then come back. Staying in Auckland or Sydney was not much of a difference in the scheme of things, so Em and I just decided to stay where we were. We moved into the city in the afternoon. The IRB put us up at the Sky Tower, which was pretty busy with the final on the Sunday.

On the Saturday afternoon we had lunch with some friends from Perth, who had come over for the last games. And then in the evening Em and I headed out to the racecourse to do a question-and-answer at a supporters' dinner that Will Genia had asked me to do. Dan Crowley, who was the MC, has such a sharp, quick, 'front rower' sense of humour. It was great to see the way he managed the crowd and was able to really get a laugh with his quips about almost anything. He was good at managing awkward questions from the audience as well and I liked the way he went about it.

One guy started his question with, 'I'm from Melbourne, and Scotland before that' and Dan said straight away, 'same shit weather'. The crowd loved him and it made it pretty painless. Sometimes they can go on for ages and the questions can be pretty uncomfortable.

One guy in the crowd stood up and was talking about how he'd been to every World Cup since 1987 and this was the first time he'd experienced hate (in the soccer rivals' sense) at one. He said one of the things he's always loved about rugby is the camaraderie and good on-field and off-field attitudes, and after being in New Zealand and experiencing the real animosity of the New Zealand public and media towards the Australian team he was concerned about what would happen to the game. The crowd and the dinner wasn't particularly responsive to his comments so he got cut off part way through, but I found it really interesting. Especially in light of the conversation I'd had with the French touring group in the pool. It was very noticeable that we had been the team that was singled out as 'the enemy', with Quade even being referred to in the papers as 'public enemy number one'. At games he was booed and when he went down looking injured in both the USA pool game and the game against Wales, the crowd erupted into cheers. I've never seen that kind of attitude before. Em was telling me about some articles she had read in the local papers that have talked about how we're (the Wallabies) so much more 'arrogant, brash and abrasive' than the other teams. It's lucky none of the guys really read the press because that kind of stuff can be really disheartening, even though we know not to take it too seriously.

I woke up early on World Cup final day to do some Heroes and EightyTwenty work, and worked through until about 2:30PM when Em and I managed to do a workout in our hotel room—she did push-ups, sit-ups, burpees, bench dips while I just did some rehab stuff for my back, exercises the physios wanted me to do. Then at 3:30PM Morgan, my best friend from Brisbane schooldays, and his girlfriend Anne arrived. Em had called them the day before to say we had a couple of spare tickets to the final and did they want to come over. Anne had arrived in Sydney, having left her passport in Toowoomba, but they still managed to get here. So we had some food and then got picked up for the game. I'd been invited to go and watch the game in the DHL corporate box and do a question and answer with Tana Umaga, Serge Betsen, Sean Fitzpatrick and Stu Wilson. It was a pretty fun night—I loved getting to meet Tana and see Serge. We also bumped into Francois Pienaar in the parking lot. After he left I whispered to Em, 'Em, that was Francois Pienaar!', She whispered back, 'Cool, who's Francois Pienaar?' Morgan and the DHL guys were pretty amused. Needless to say, she's never watched *Invictus* and her pre-2009 rugby knowledge is fairly limited.

The game was very close and the French had clearly turned up to play. There were a lot of very nervous All Blacks after Aaron Cruden went down with a knee injury. Thierry Dusautoir, the French captain and blindside flanker, had an absolute blinder. It seemed like he was everywhere on the field. It really was a remarkable performance and just goes to show the kind of leader he is. The French also lost their No. 10 but managed to hang in. I really thought they were going to win until the last few minutes. I was near Serge Betsen and Tana Umaga and seeing the apprehension and excitement on both their faces was pretty exciting. Despite my excitement at getting to meet some of the heroes of the game and the fun of having Morgan and Anne there, it was a pretty miserable experience. It's not fun to watch a game you think you could have played in. It was eighty minutes for me to think about all the things that happened that stopped us from getting there and all the years of hard work that had led me to be watching the game from the sidelines rather than being out on the field.

After the game we went on to a function at the Viaduct. It was packed and you could see it was just going to get busier and more wild, so Morgs, Anne, Em and I headed back to the hotel and hung out and chatted until they caught a cab to the airport at 4AM.

We slept in the next morning and spent the day holed up in the hotel room working on the book and avoiding the ticker-tape parade happening outside. At 6:30PM we met Robbie, Digby, Radike, Will and James Horwill, who'd all flown back in for the IRB awards night. It was being held at the Vector Arena and there were about 1200 people there. It was a pretty long evening. Radike and Digby had both been nominated for Try of the Year, and Will and I had both been nominated for IRB Player of the Year, along with Ma'a Nonu, Jerome Kaino and Piri Weepu from the All Blacks and the French captain Thierry Dusautoir. I was nominated last year as well and Richie McCaw went on to claim the award.

It's a huge award—IRB Player of the Year. This year it was being voted on by a panel of former players, including the likes of John Eales, Francois Pienaar, Tana Umaga and Augustin Pichot. They had weighted it so that the World Cup games counted for a lot more than the other internationals. That was always going to make it very difficult for me to win, having missed two of the pool games after injuring my back. I still had a glimmer of hope though that this would be some sort of consolation after our disappointing result, but after watching France play the All Blacks the night before and seeing Thierry Dusautoir's performance it seemed much more likely that he would take the honours.

After Radike took the prize for Try of the Year and George Smith was awarded the IRPA Special Merit Award, it was already a good year for Australian rugby in terms of the awards. New Zealand claimed Coach of the Year and also Team of the Year and then Thierry Dusautoir was named IRB Player of the Year. He made a beautiful speech, which really exemplified the kind of man and player he is, ending with an address to his team in French. While I'm sure he'd have exchanged it in a flash to have been holding the Webb Ellis Cup, it must have been a bitter-sweet moment.

Even though I had thought that Dusautoir would win, and even though it was a thoroughly deserved award, I still felt really disappointed. I was surprised by how disappointed I felt. I think I had underestimated the emotional toll the year had taken on me. I don't play for personal awards—I'm not sure many guys do, because it'd be a pretty unsustainable motivation—but that kind of recognition from a group of your peers is really significant. But it wasn't to be again this year. From the moment we left the dinner my disappointment started to subside a little and it made me more determined to one day win that award, and also win a Rugby World Cup. We have all learnt a lot from this experience, and for those of us that know we may have another shot at it, the preparations for England in 2015 started the moment we lost to the All Blacks in the semi-final.

# Reflections

*What you keep to yourself you lose,*
*what you give away, you keep forever.*
Axel Munthe

Well, if you have made it this far you have almost finished reading my book. I'd like to thank you for sharing part of my story thus far and I really hope you have enjoyed it. I'm now back in Perth with time to contemplate the World Cup experience and put the finishing touches to this manuscript before it goes to the printer.

Writing this book has been a huge undertaking, and at times hard to fit in among my other commitments, but has been an enriching experience and I have enjoyed it for the most part.

I left New Zealand on the Tuesday pretty disappointed with how things had gone. I'd say that would be the same for most of the team. We had some great times but ultimately our loss to Ireland made it a tougher route to the final and we weren't good enough in the semi-final against the eventual winners New Zealand. We have learnt a lot about ourselves as individuals and as a team, and it has made us determined to improve, but will need to put these lessons into practice if we are to be as successful as we hope to be in the future.

I'm sitting at the Wild Fig Café, the place where I have done so much talking and reading and planning over the past four years. It shuts down this weekend after its lease was terminated. As they say, all good things must come to an end and in the disappointment there is always opportunity—and many good memories that we get to keep.

It's the end of a chapter and time to reflect on the good and the bad, to learn from them, ensuring that they form part of the motivation to improve where we can and to embrace life, living it to the full.

I'm looking forward to trips to Nkayi with Em and Luke O'Keefe for EightyTwenty Vision. I am excited about what is to come in life. I have so much more I want to do with my rugby and am determined to one day be a part of the most deserving team in the world and to win the World Cup. But it will only happen if we live in the moment and do what we can now to improve and ingrain the habits that will bring about this kind of success. It's all there to do. It's all ahead of each of us, and we get to choose how we respond to disappointments and tough times.

I am excited about developments with Heroes Boots and how they can lead to brighter futures for people in developing countries and the way we in Australia can be a part of this change. Although it is all somewhat daunting, it is something I am passionate about and believe in.

*Munhu munhu ngevanhu.* A proverb of the Shona people of Zimbabwe meaning 'a person is a person because of other people'. It is this shared humanity and care for our fellow humans that I believe is so important. A life lived for others is a life worth living and we can find fulfilment—not by accumulating more possessions or earning more money, but by having meaningful relationships with the divine and the people around us and reconnecting with the earth and the rest of humanity—giving of ourselves and working towards a world that is built on love, fairness and equality.